Hyphens

Five Senses

Holly Crawford

Lokke
New York

Photographs were taken with a Sony Cybershot camera as a project of Broadway Gallery space at Photo NY 2004   and later as a project with Brown Bag Contemporary at Photo San Francisco 2005.

www.art-poetry.info

ISBN: 978-0-9852461-5-0

Hyphens, Five Senses is a participation project at Photo NY 2004 and Photo San Francisco 2005. I asked people over the four days at each fair if I could take an image of one of their five senses. One of their senses that they thought was their strongest or the weakest. What you see was not staged. At each fair I took more than one hundred images. I printed out the photographs on 4x6 inch paper, after I took five or ten pictures, with on a very small printer and then arranged them on a wall.

see

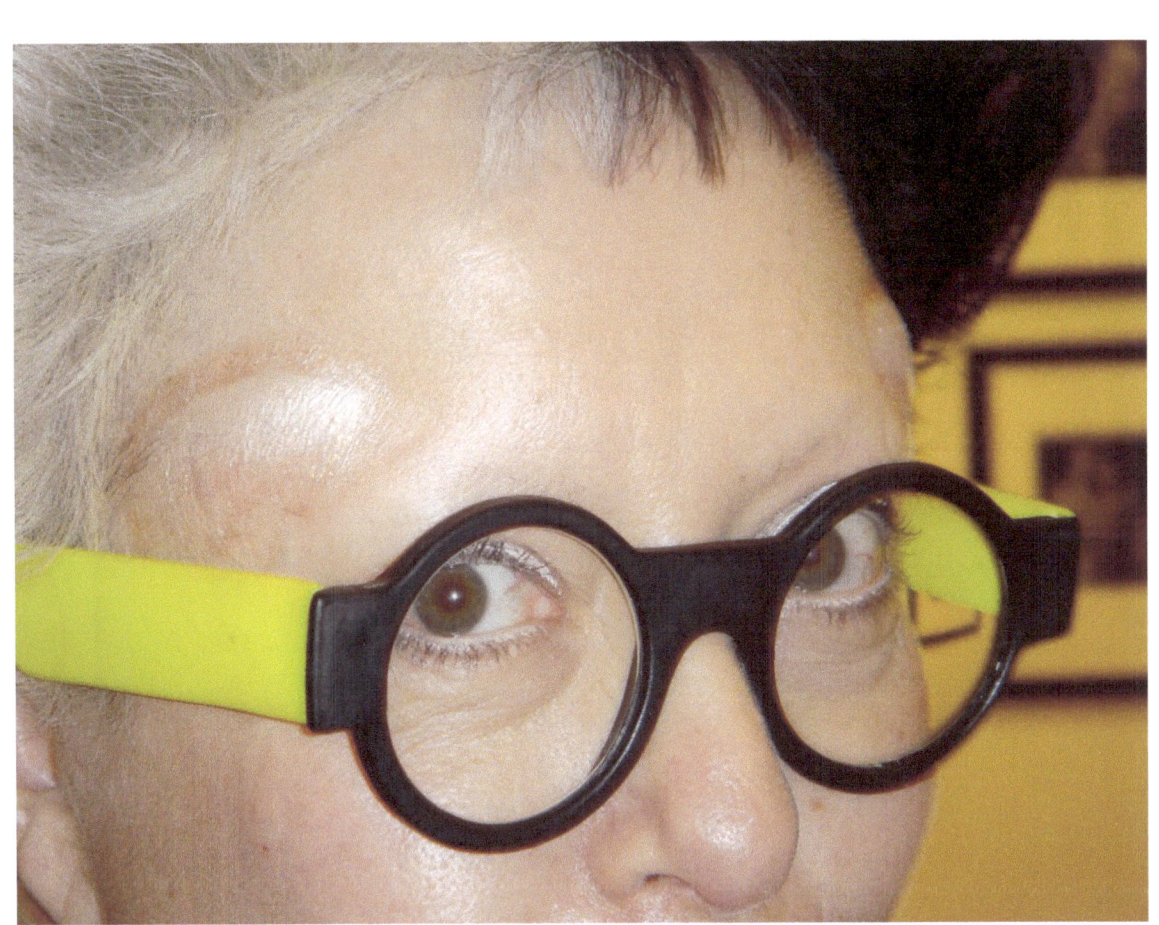

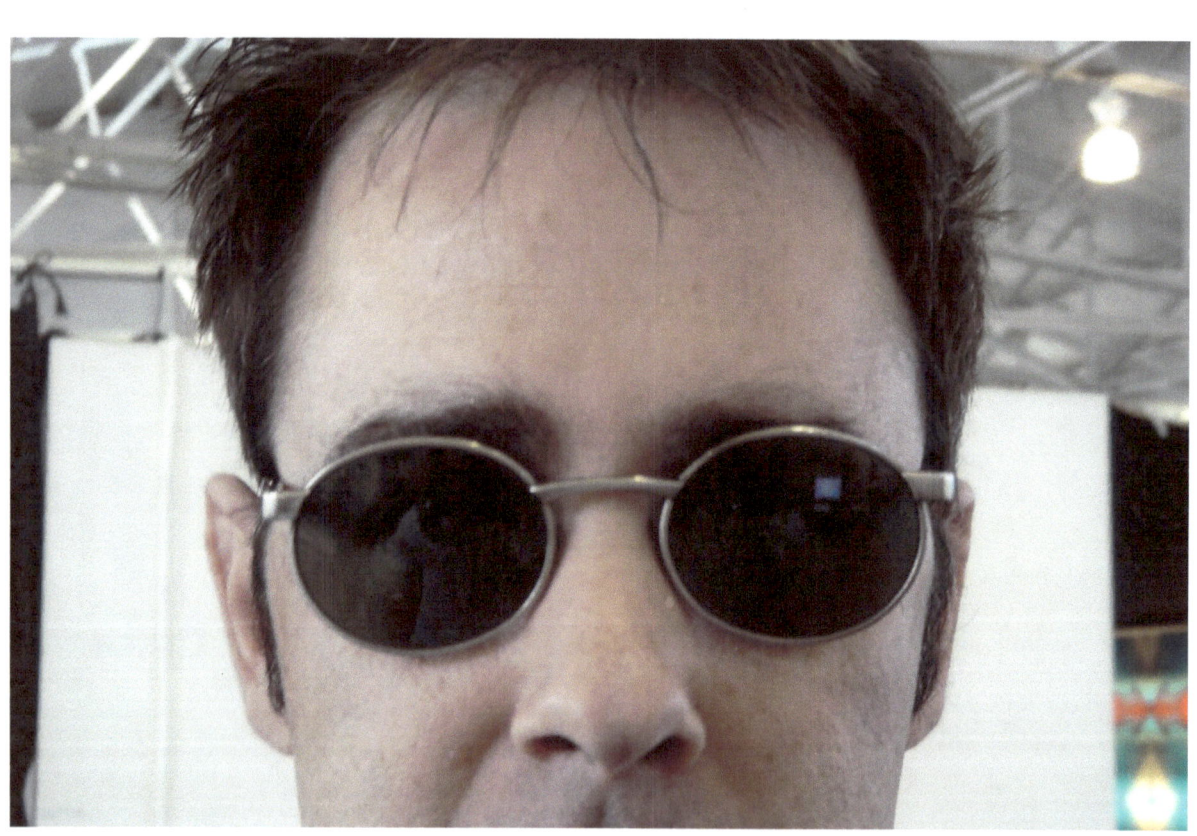

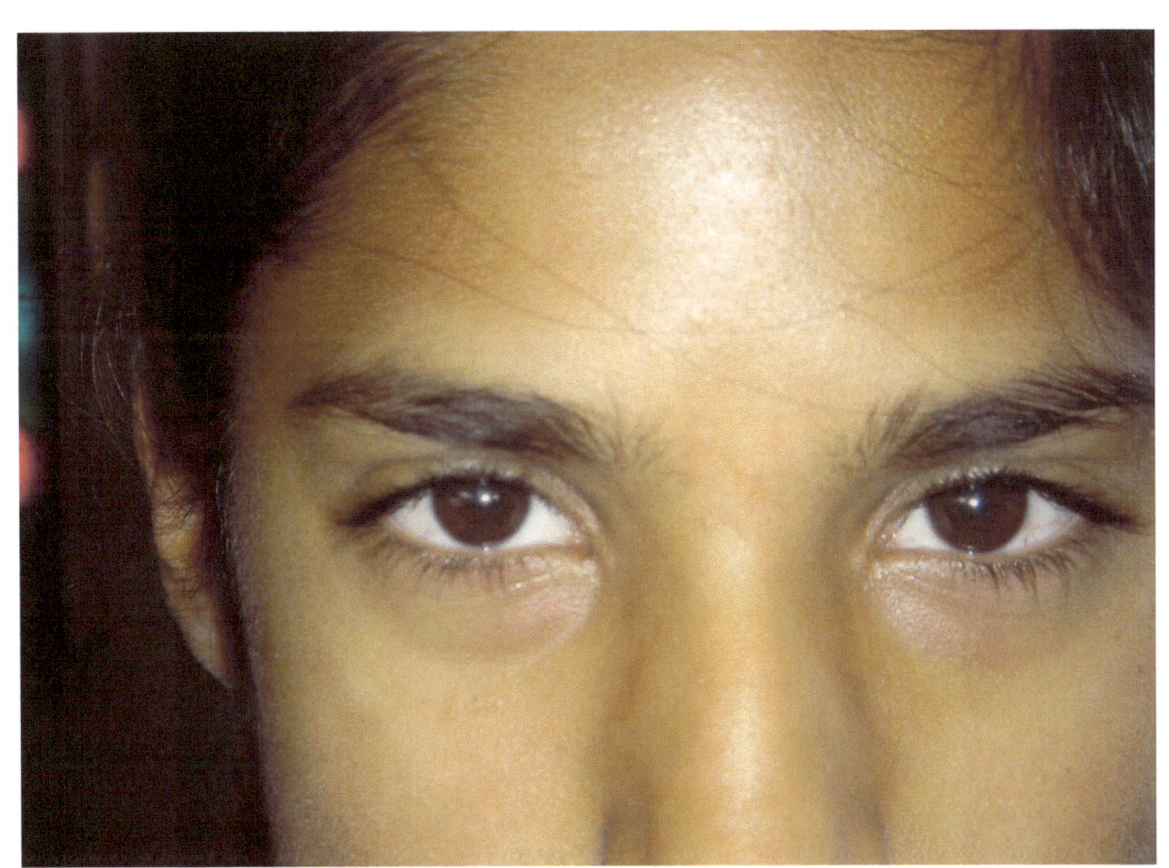

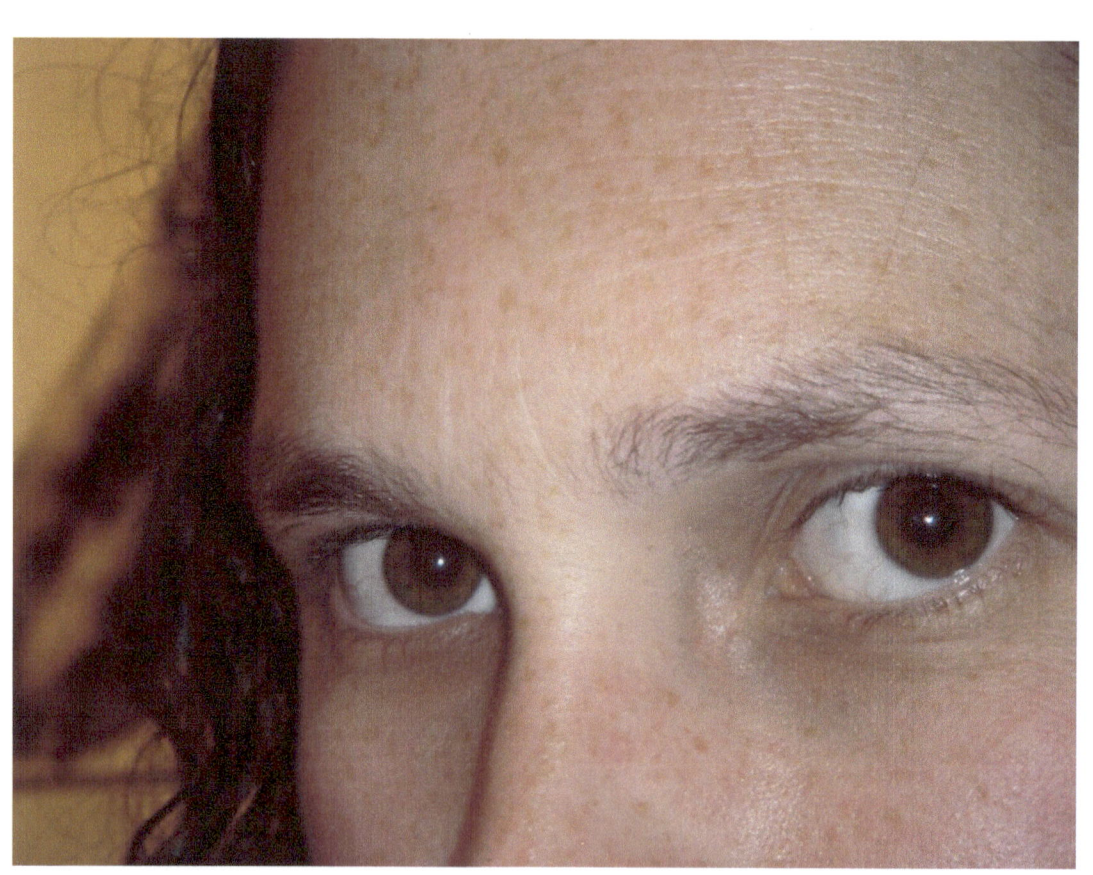

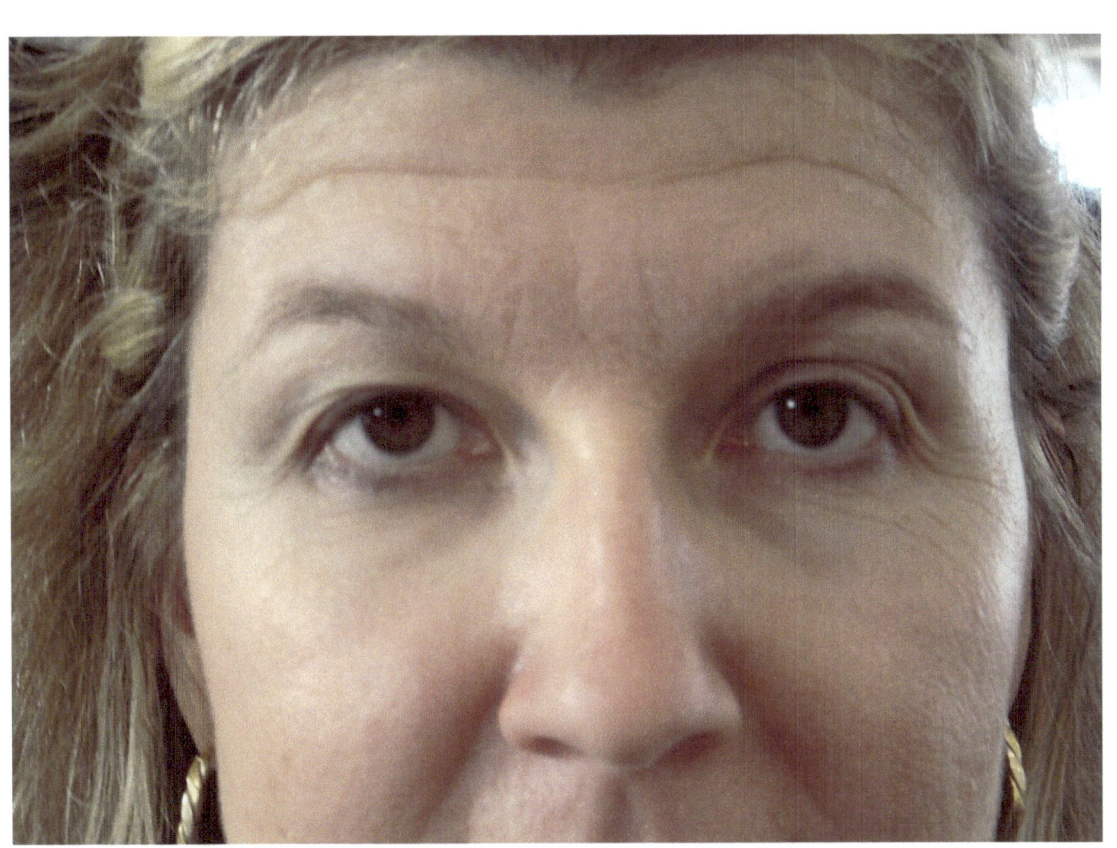

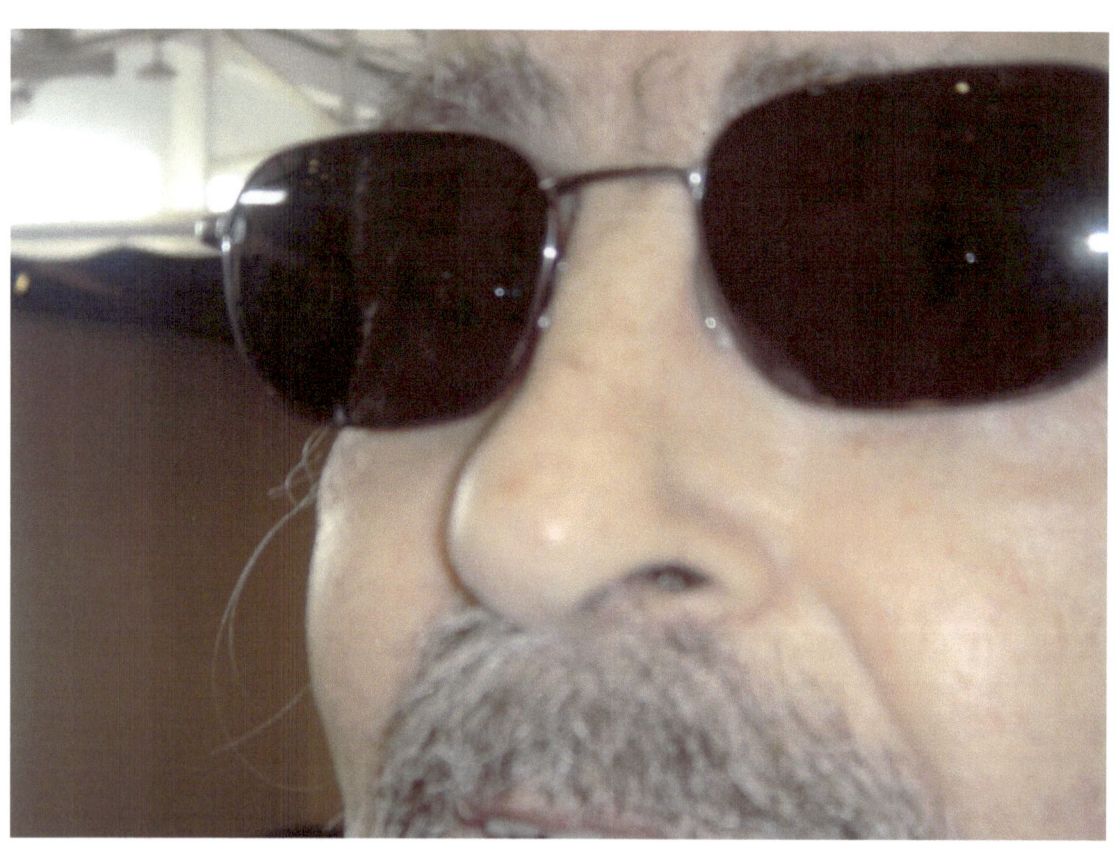

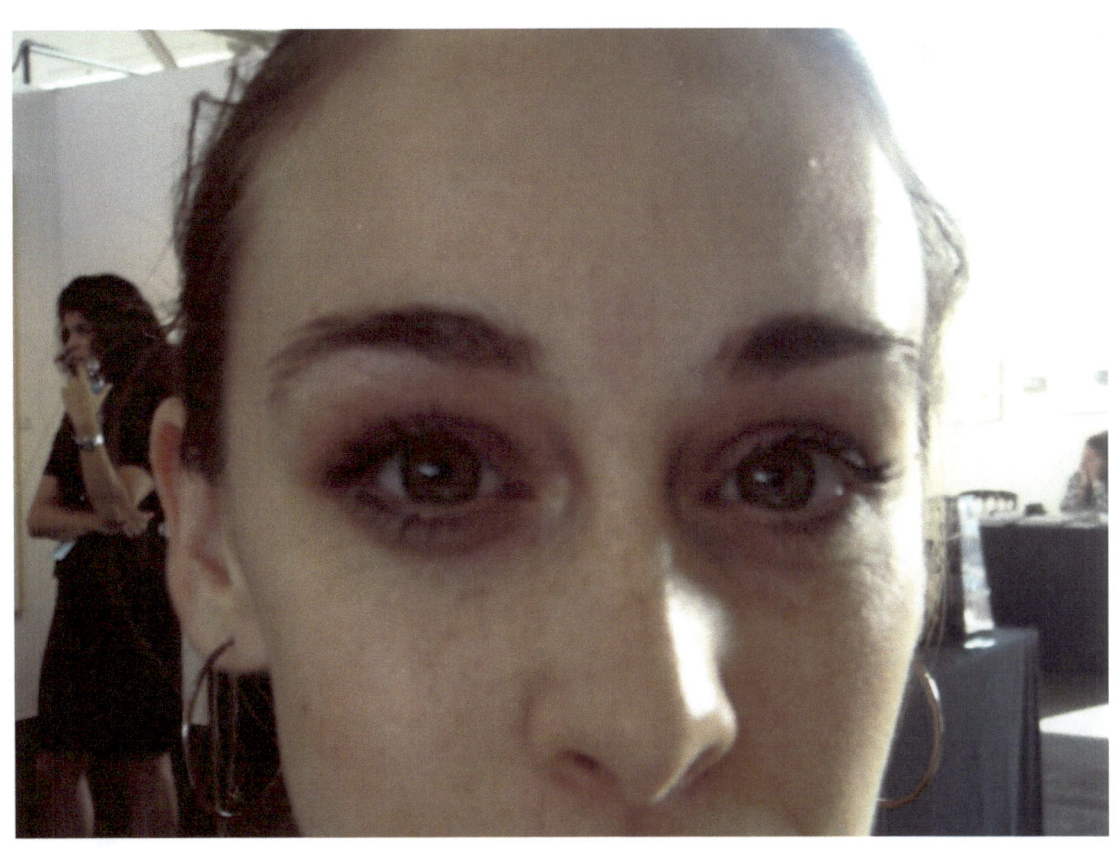

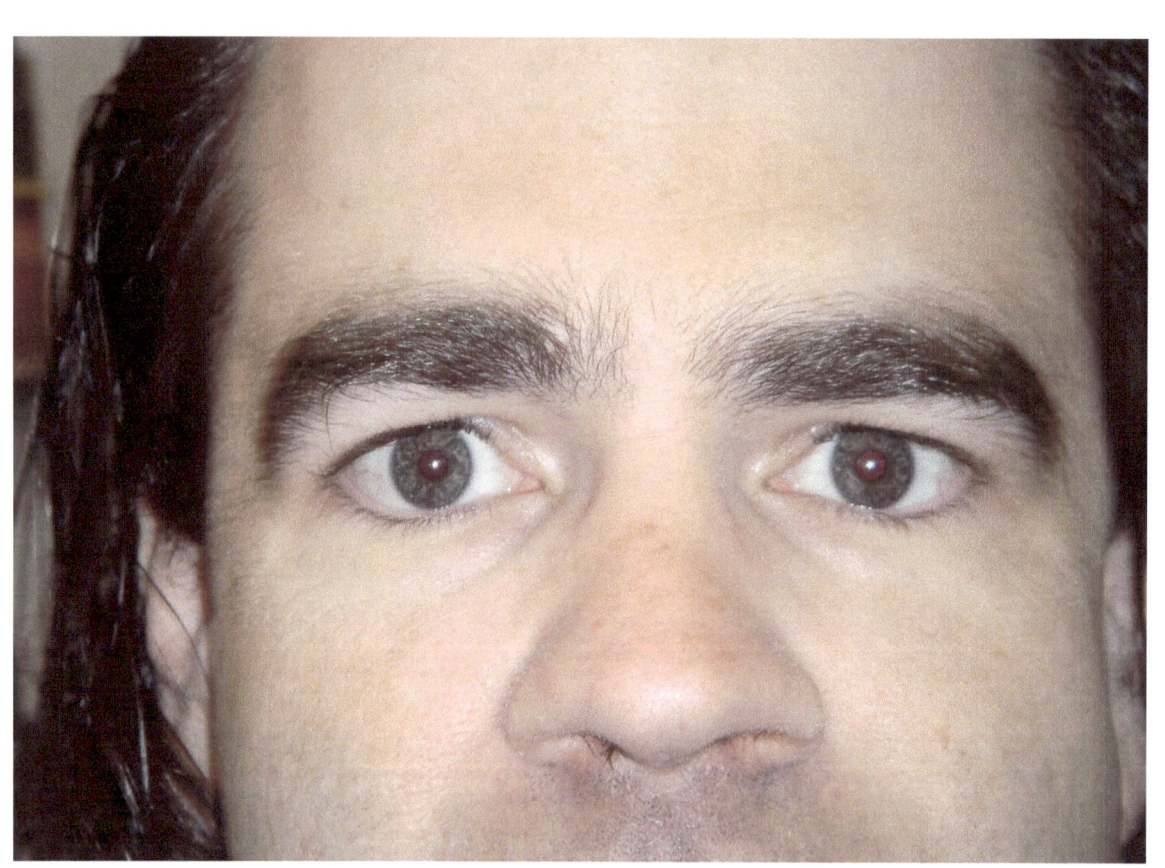

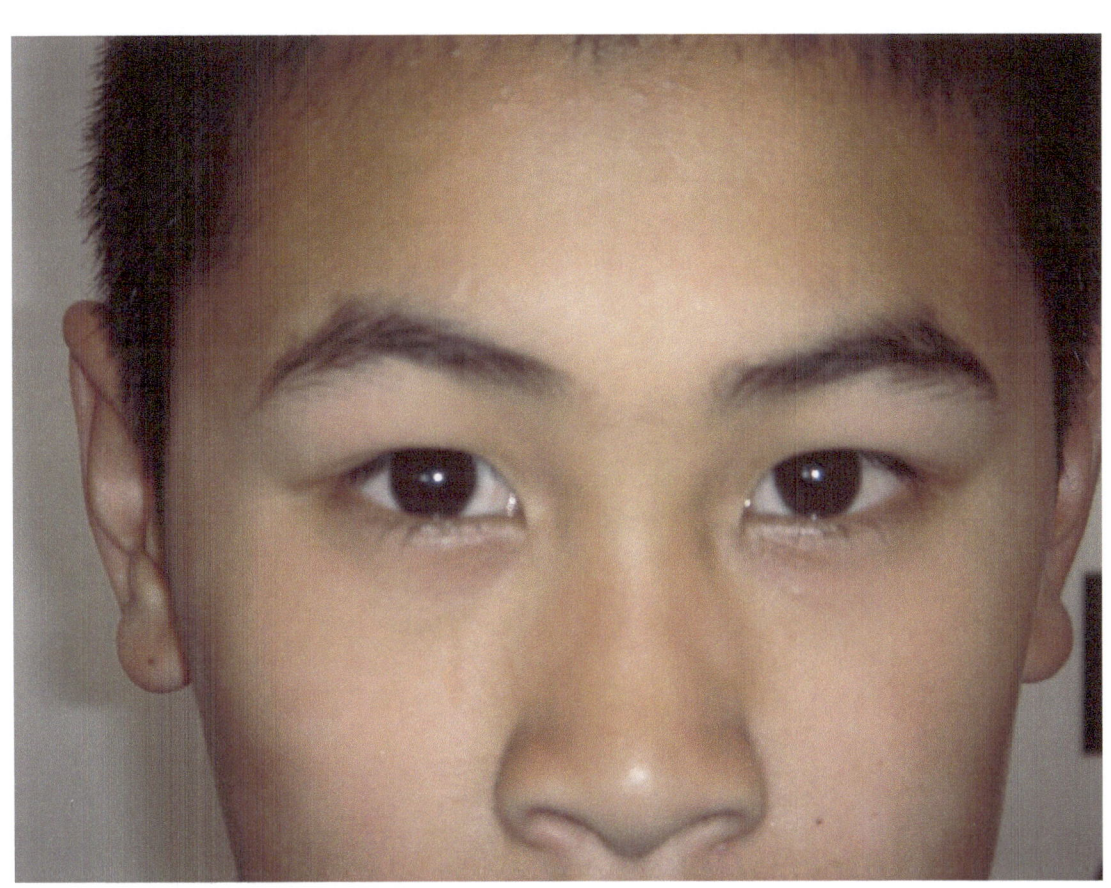

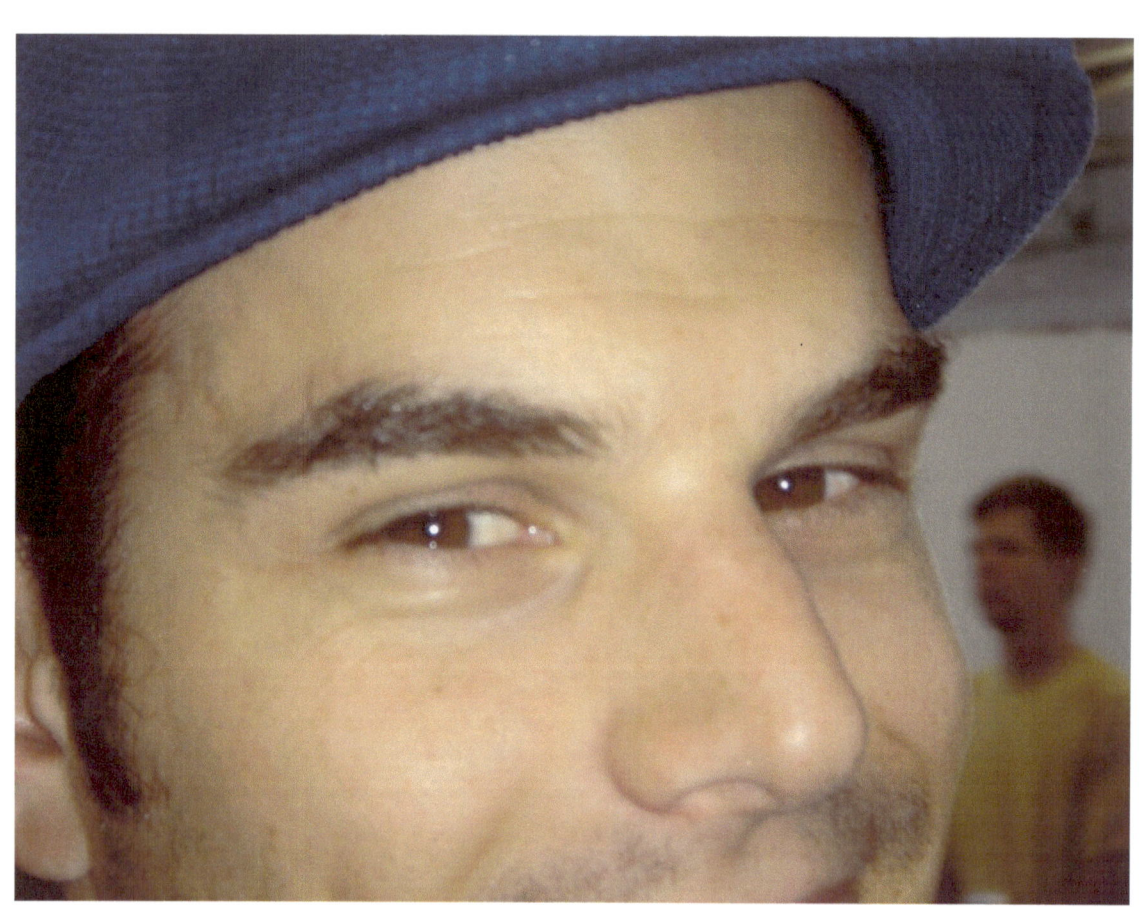

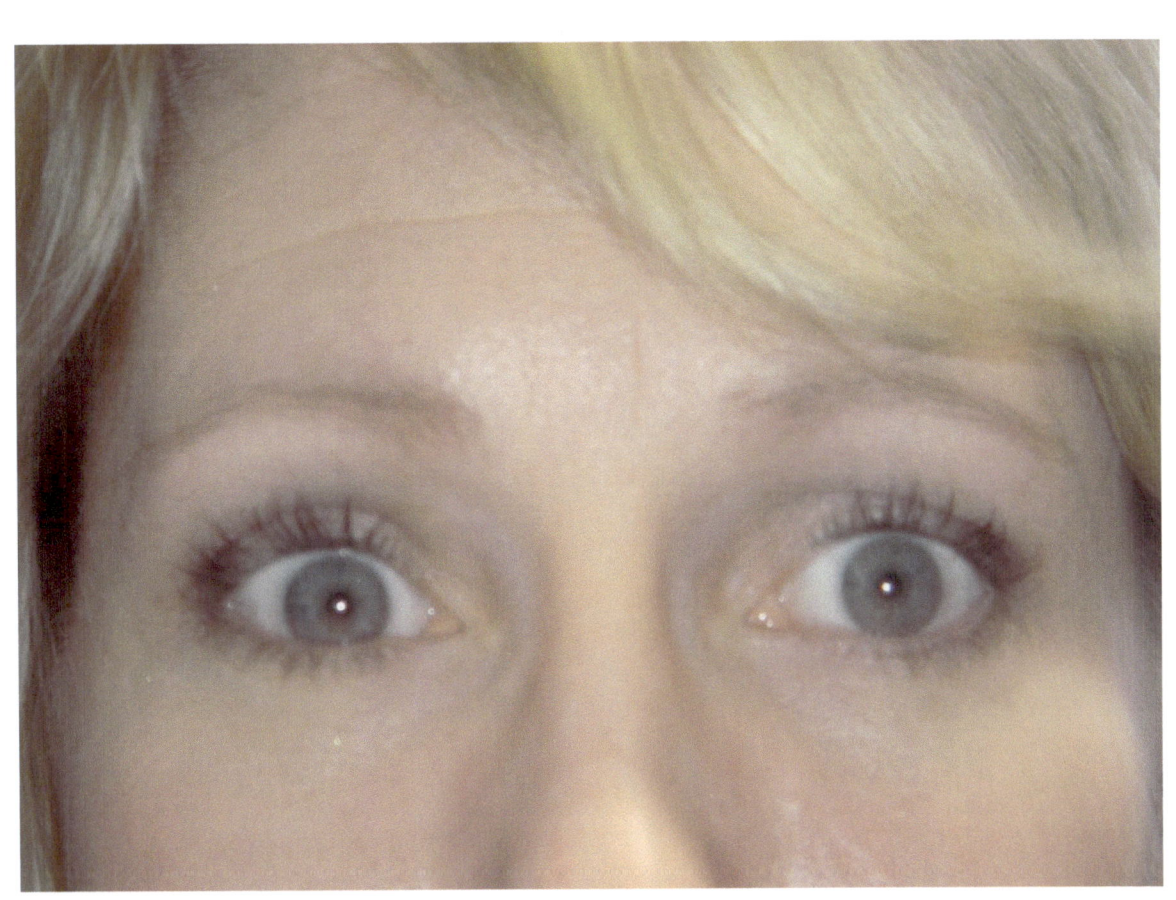

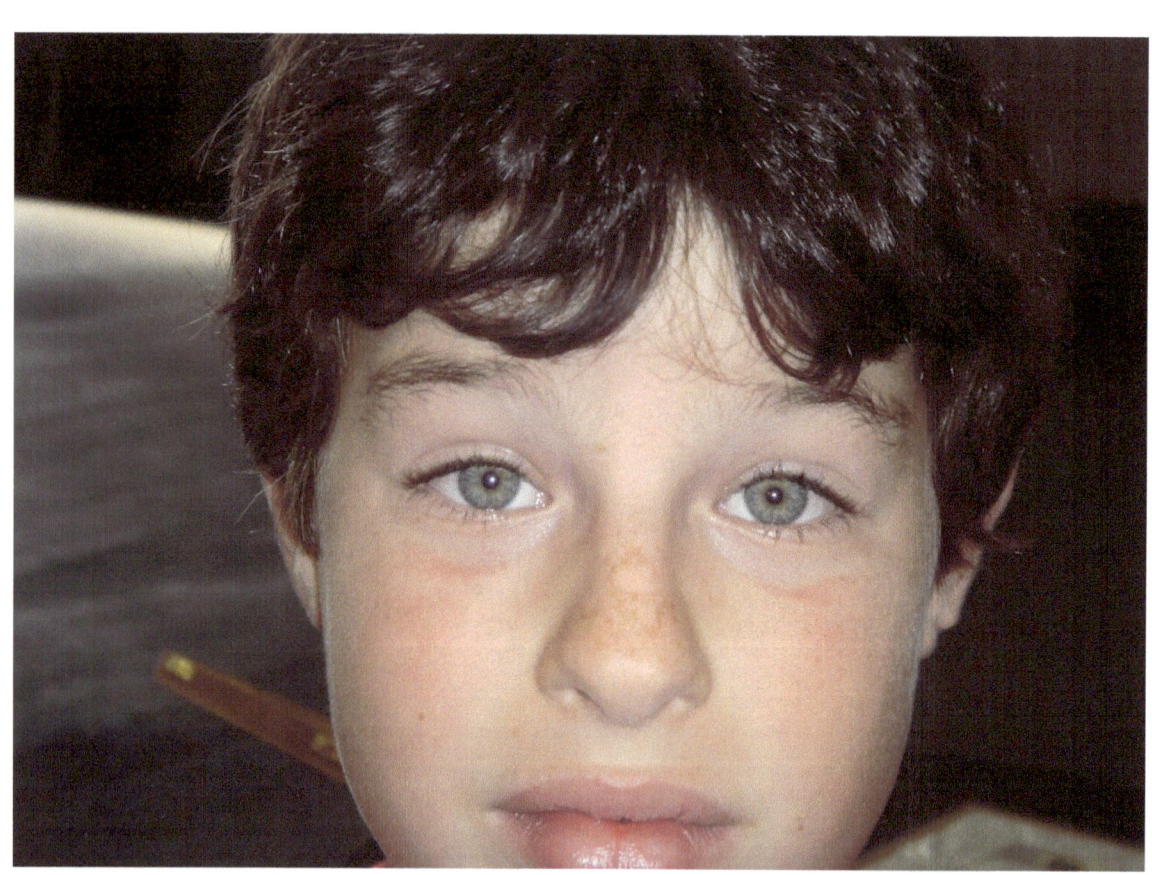

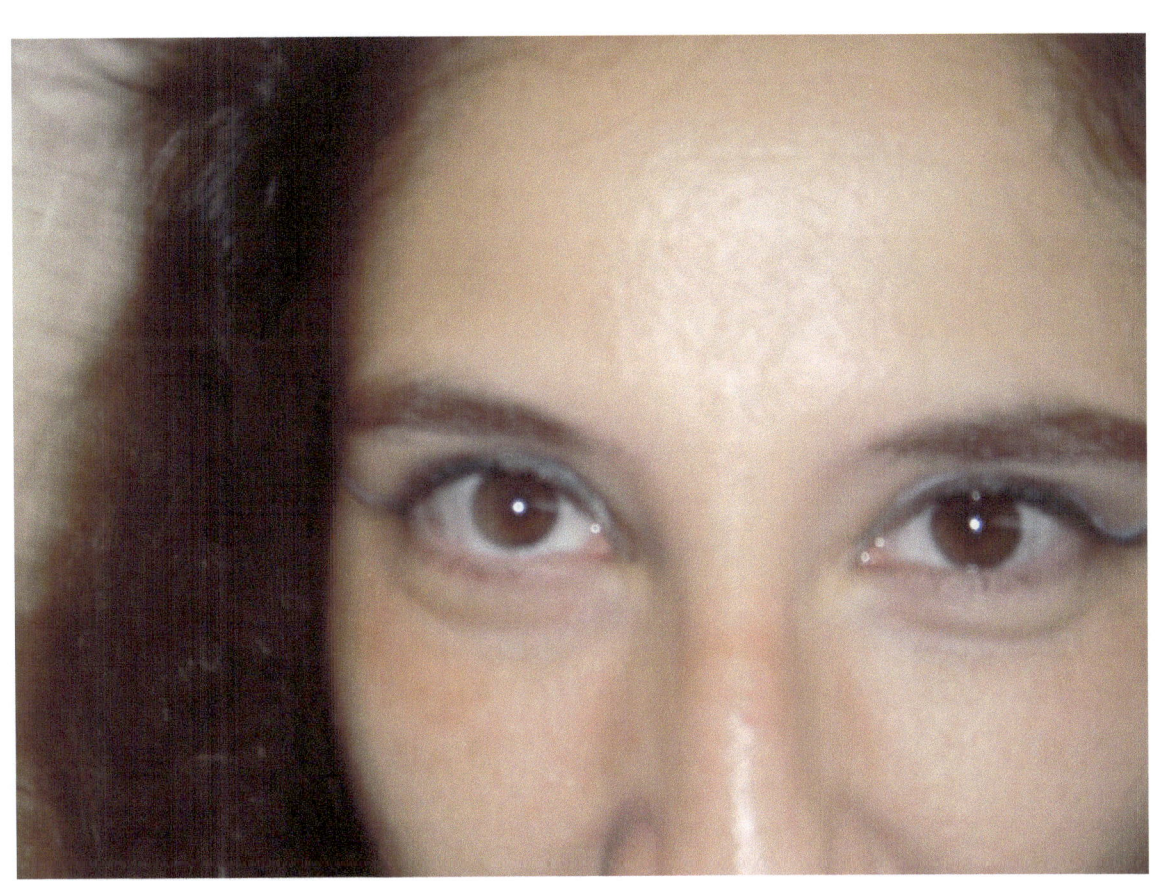

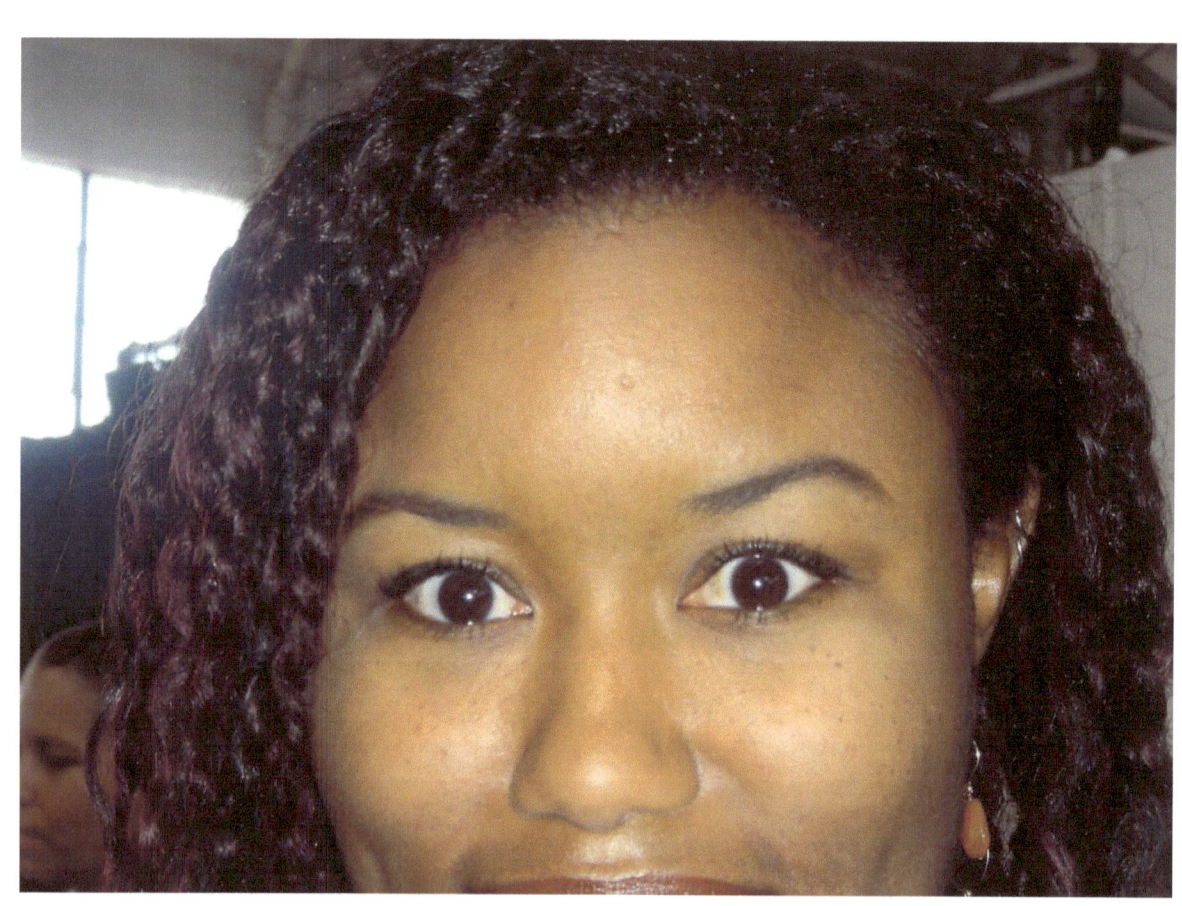

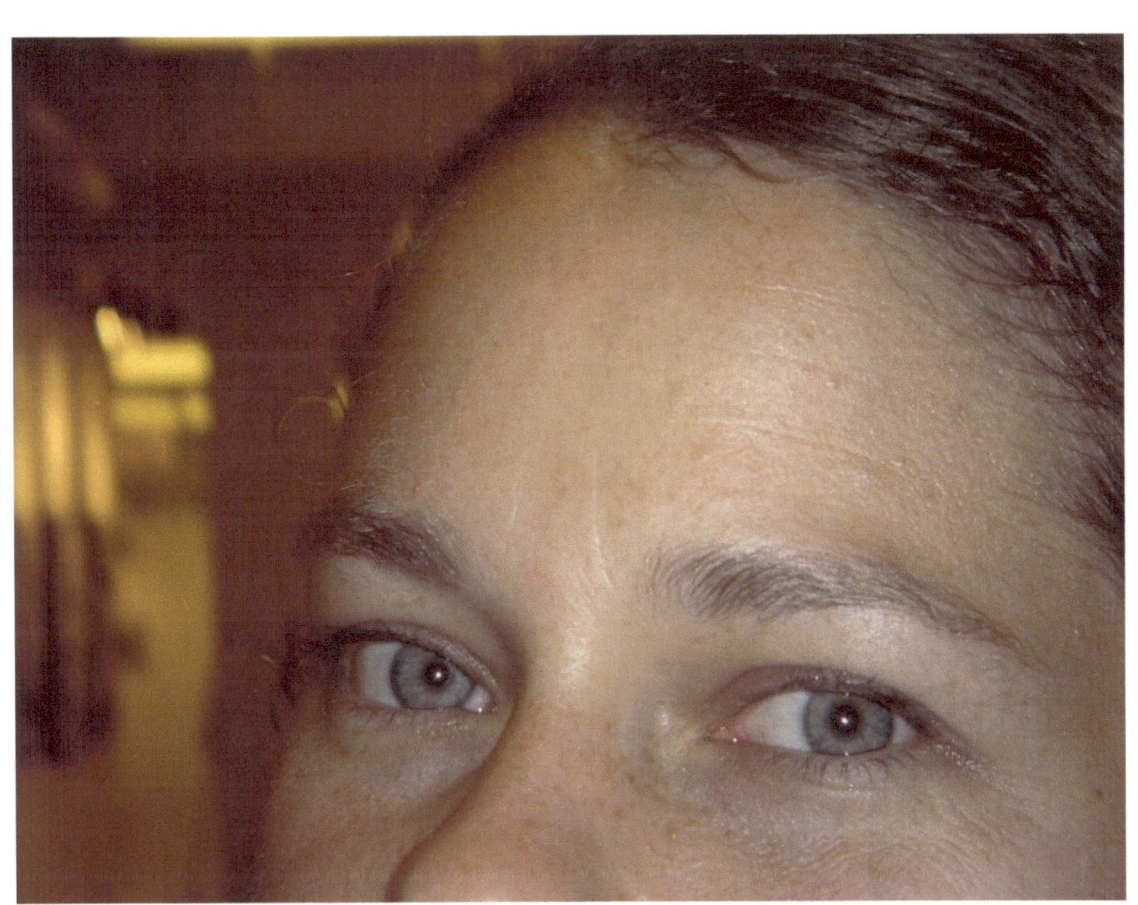

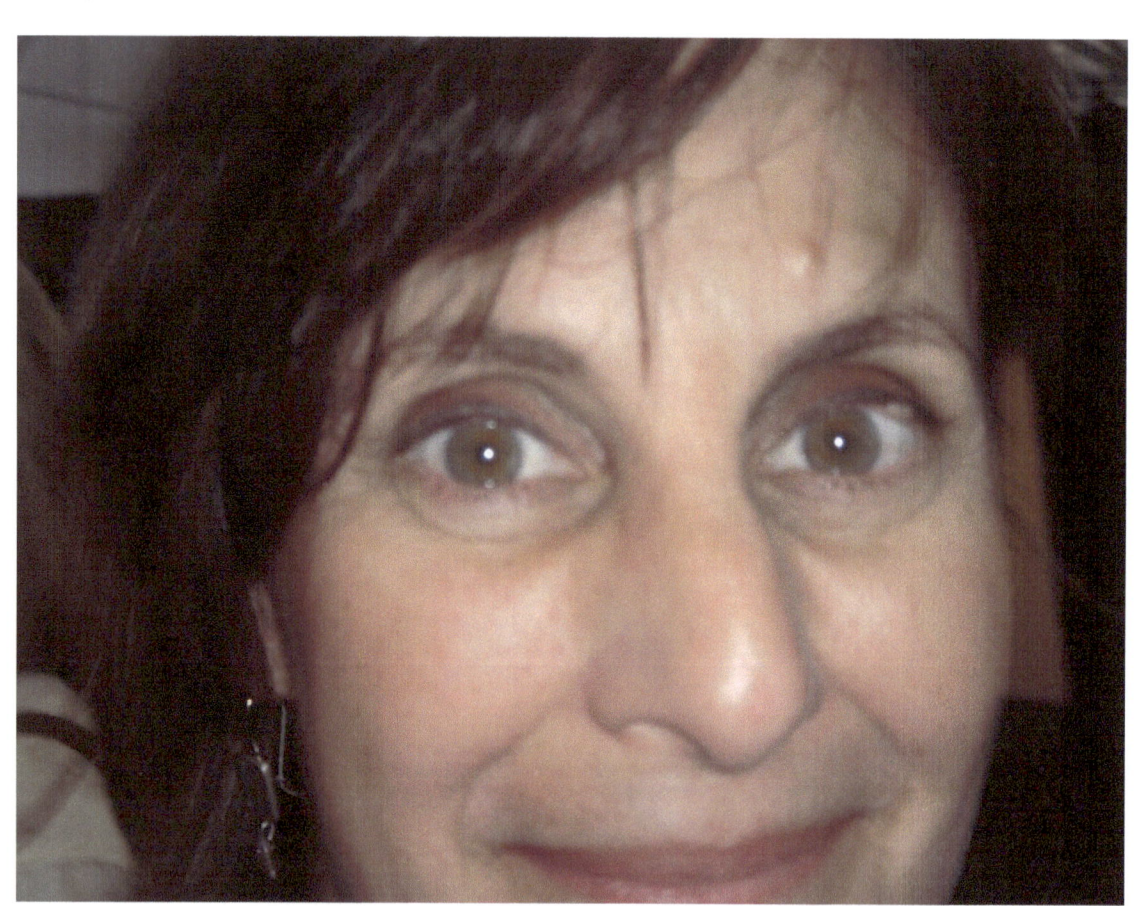

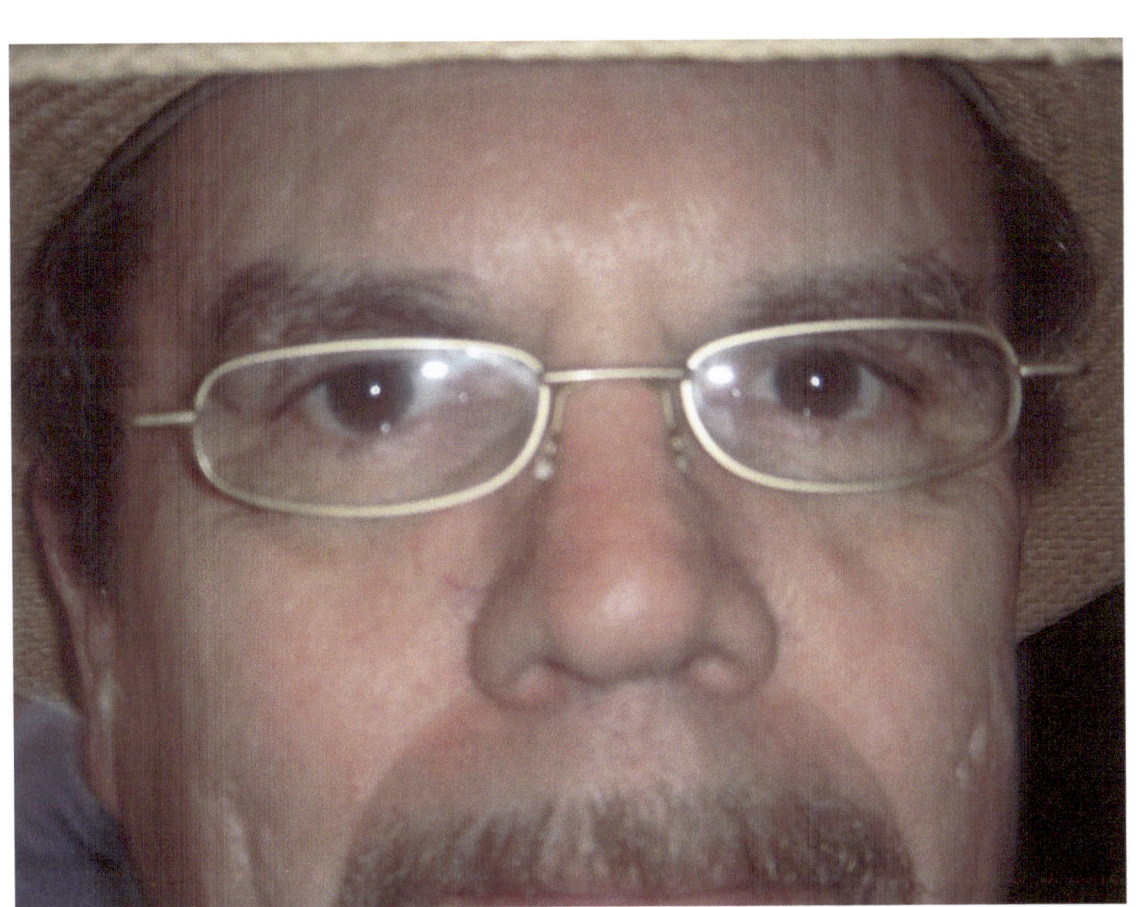

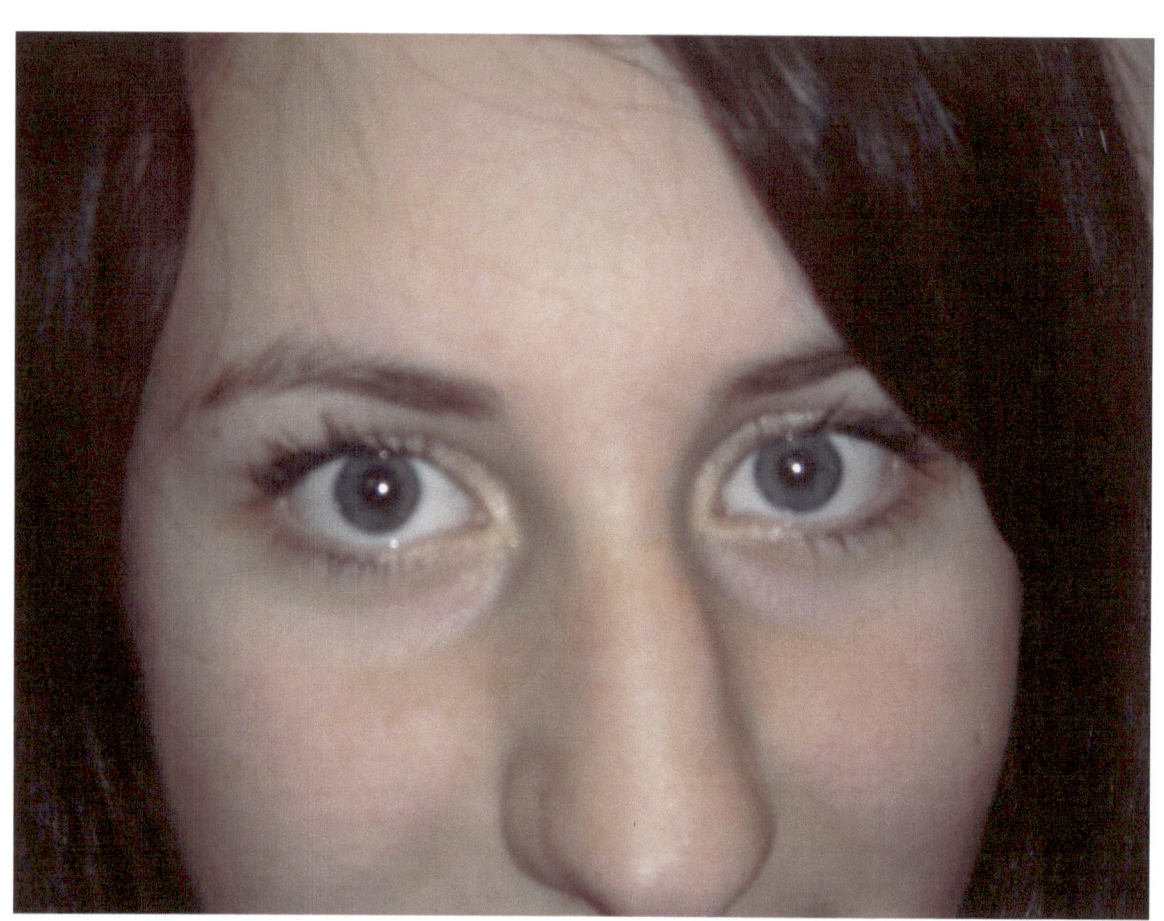

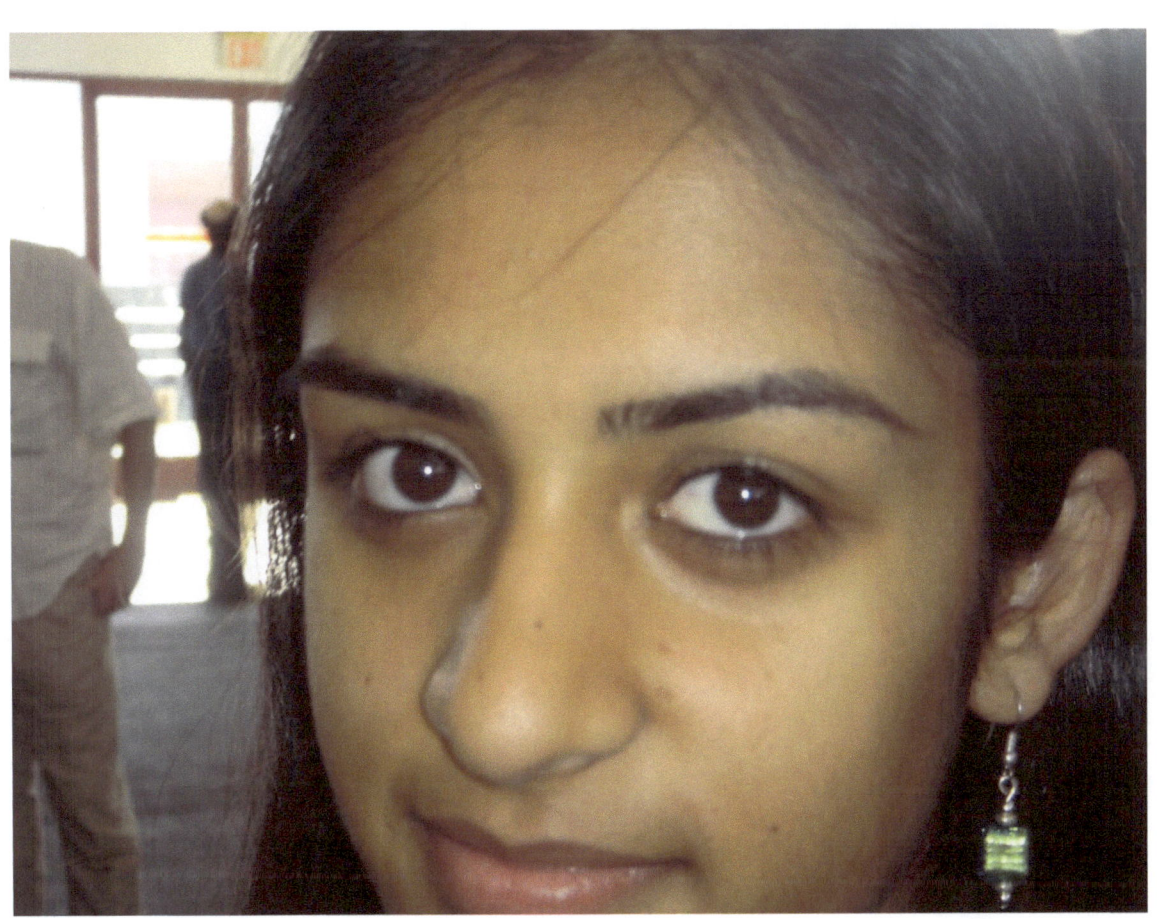

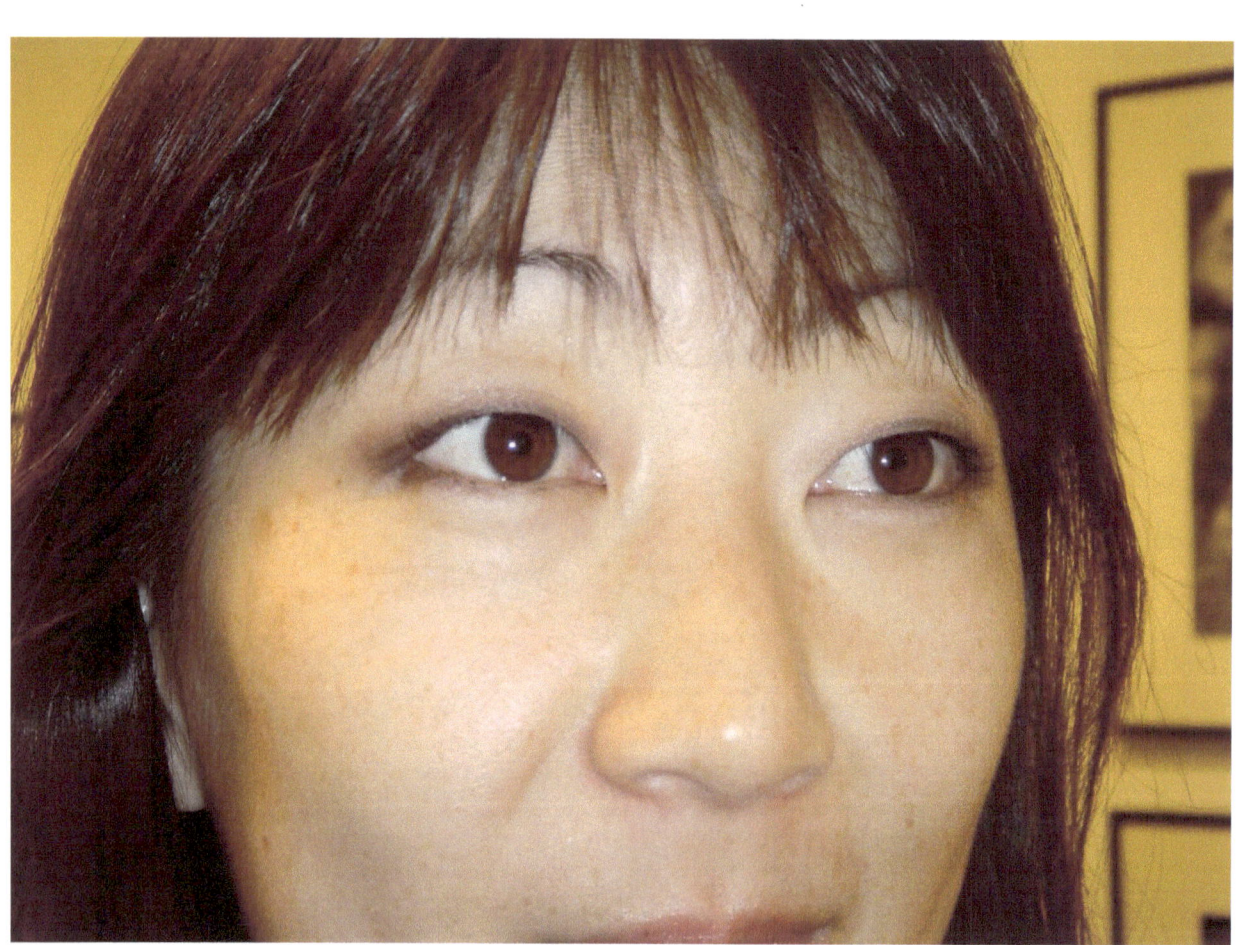

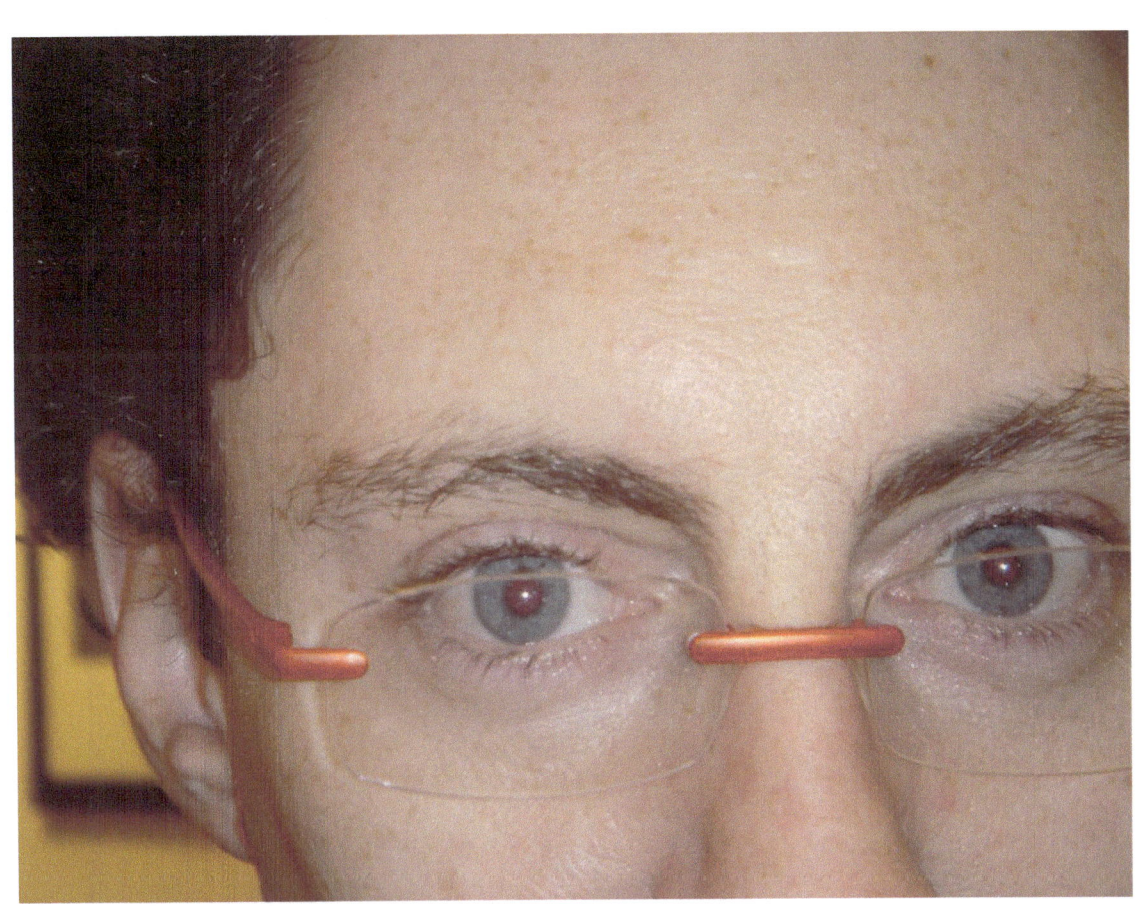

hear

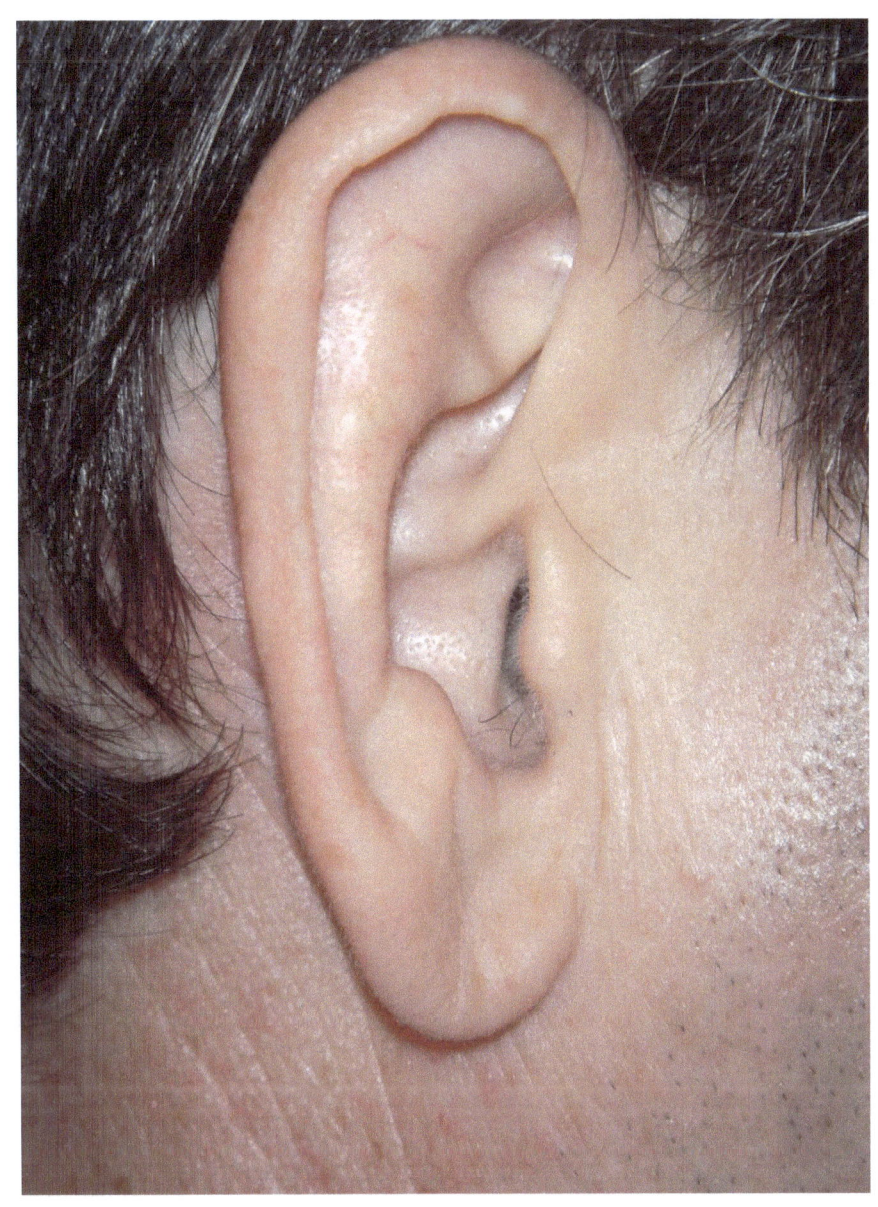

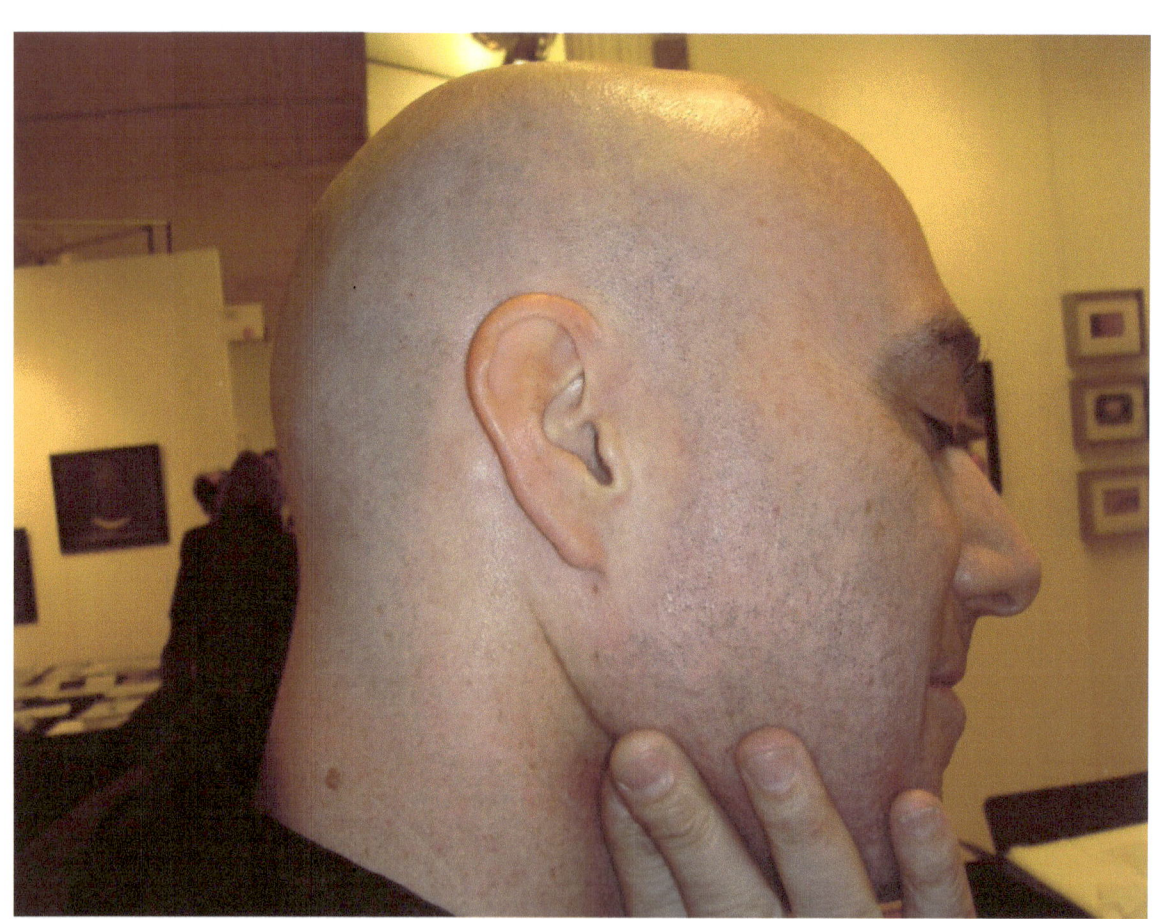

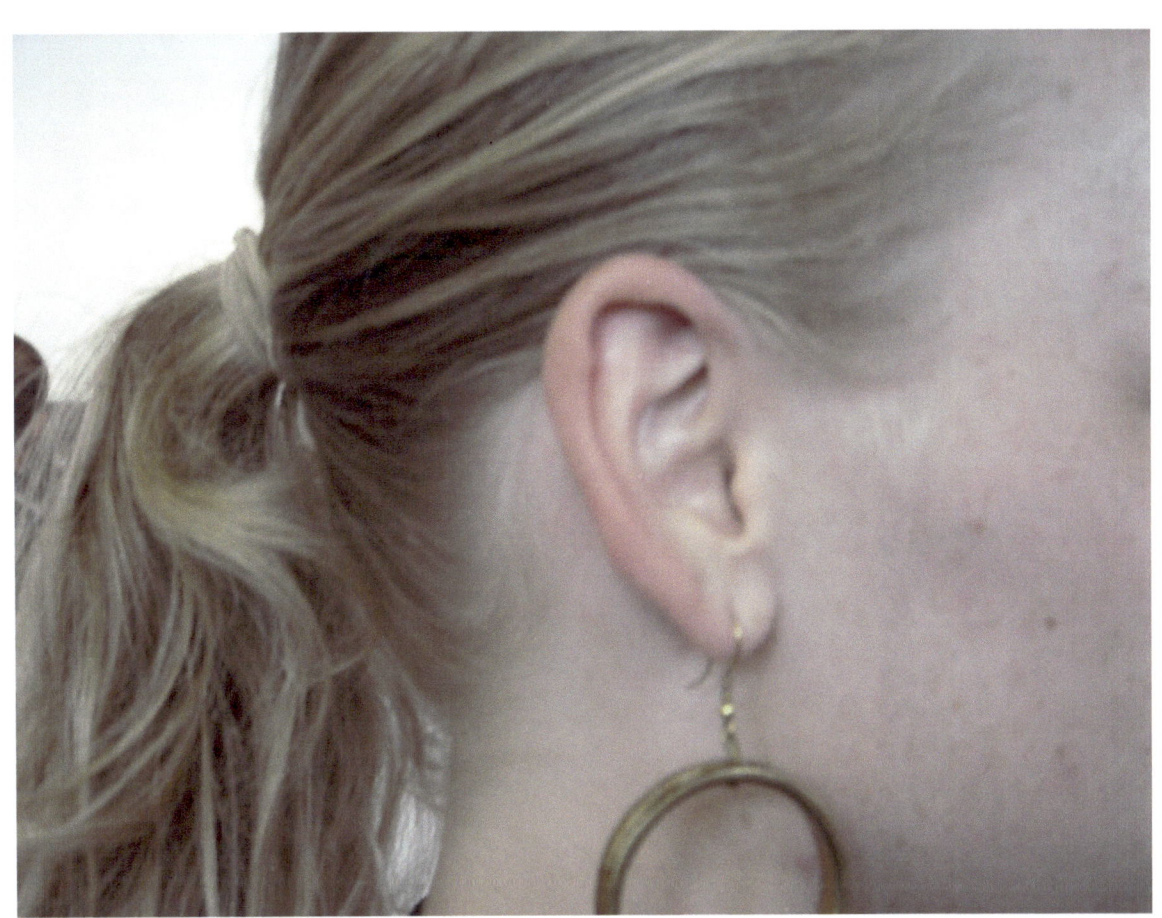

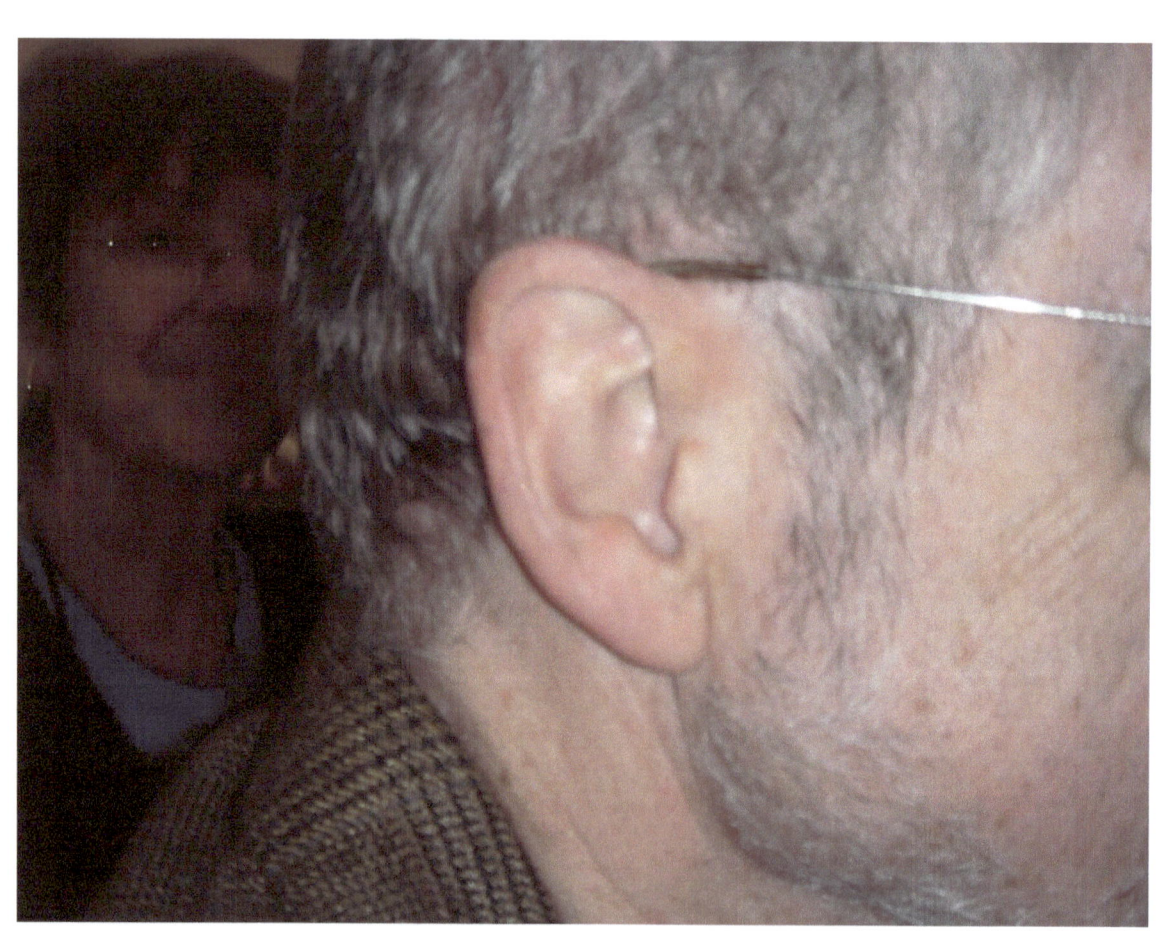

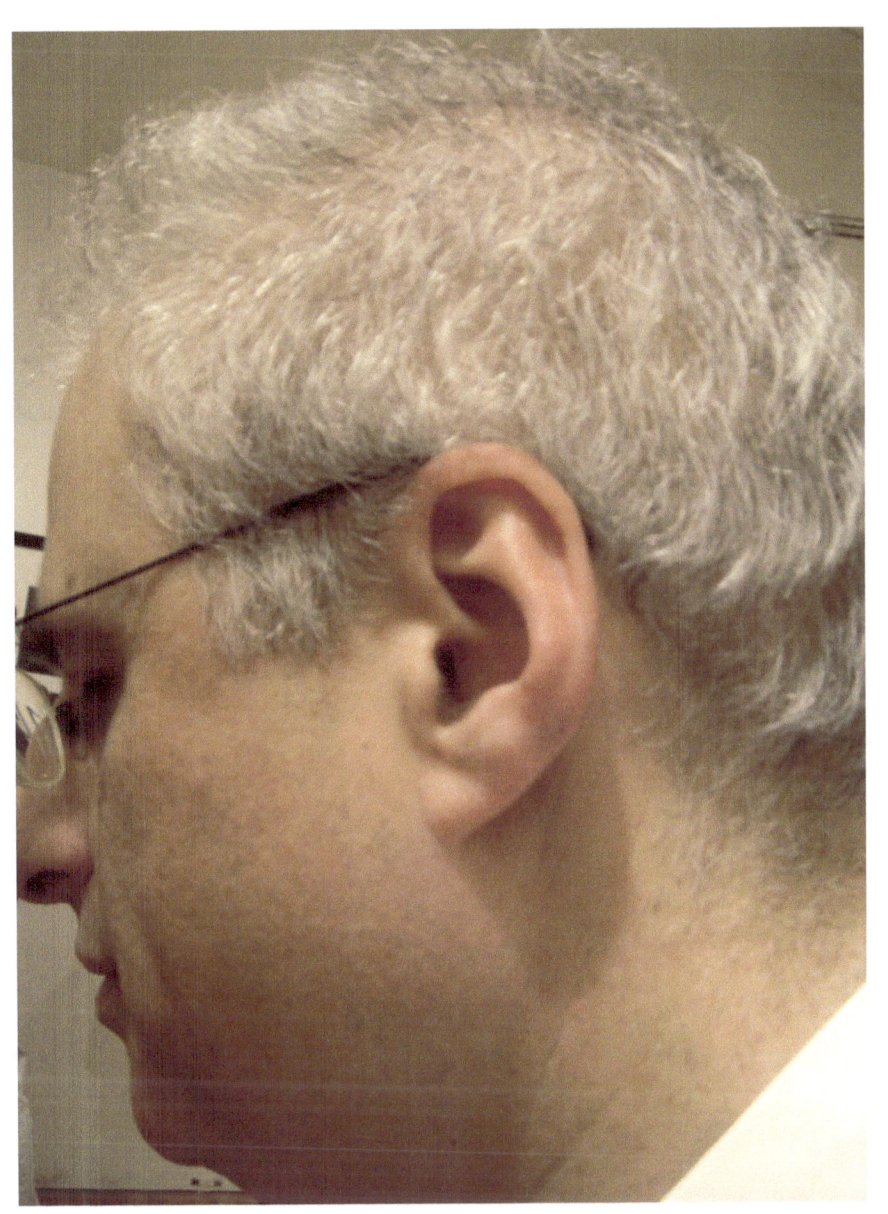

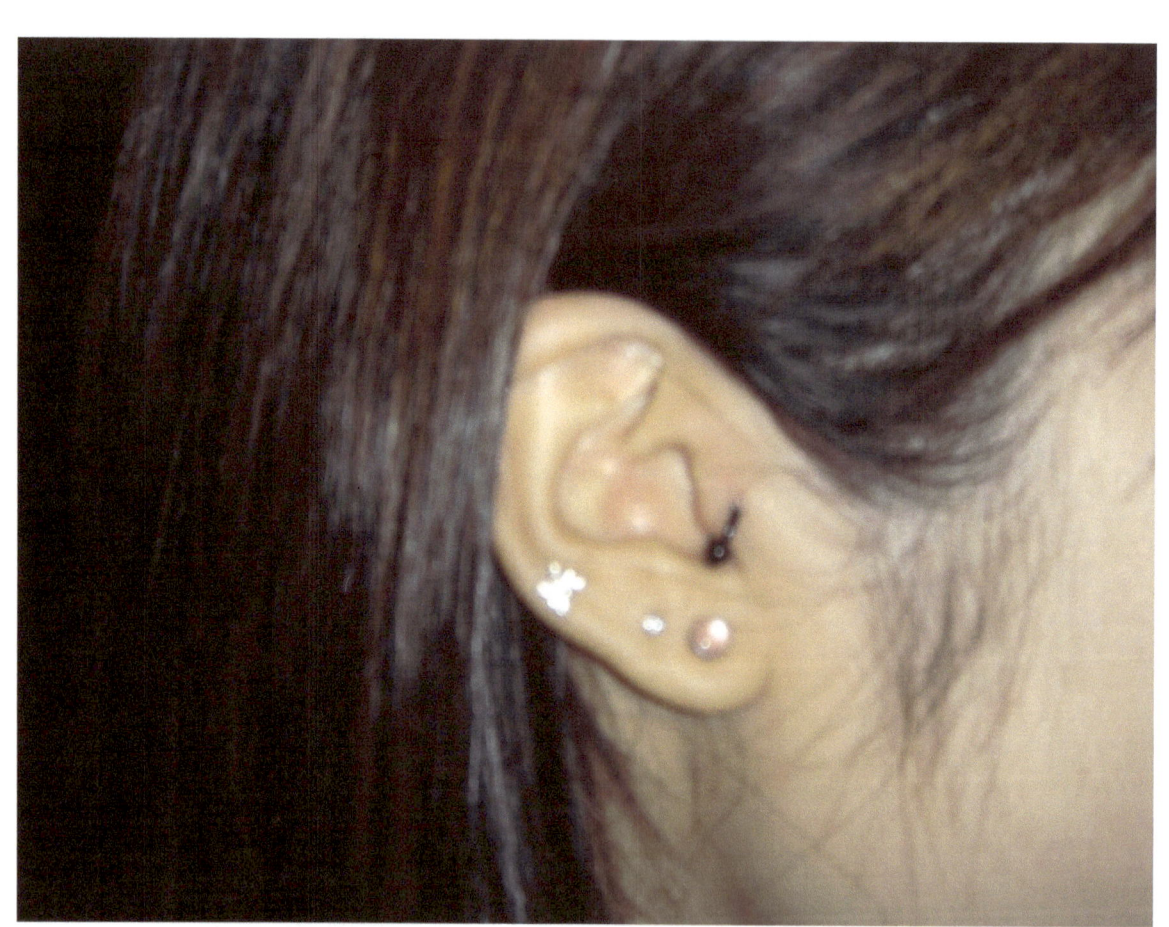

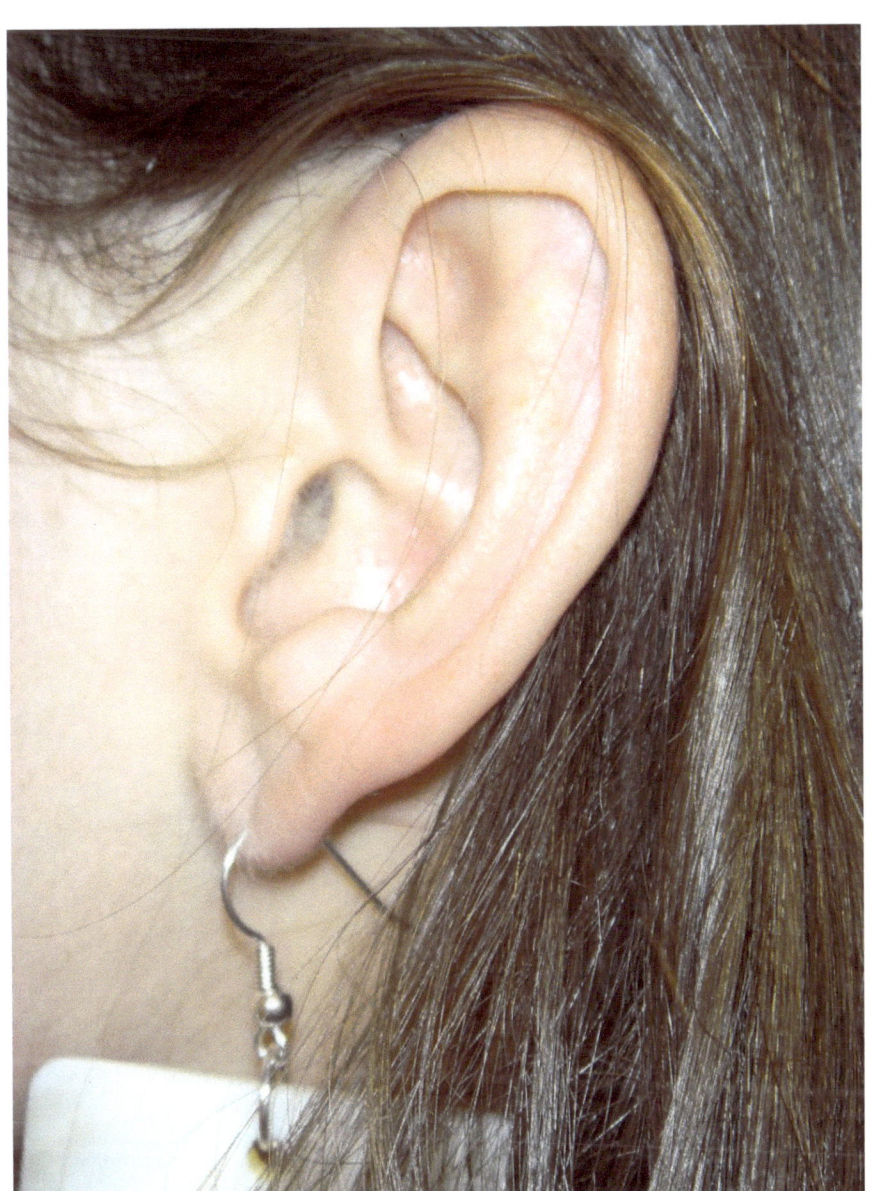

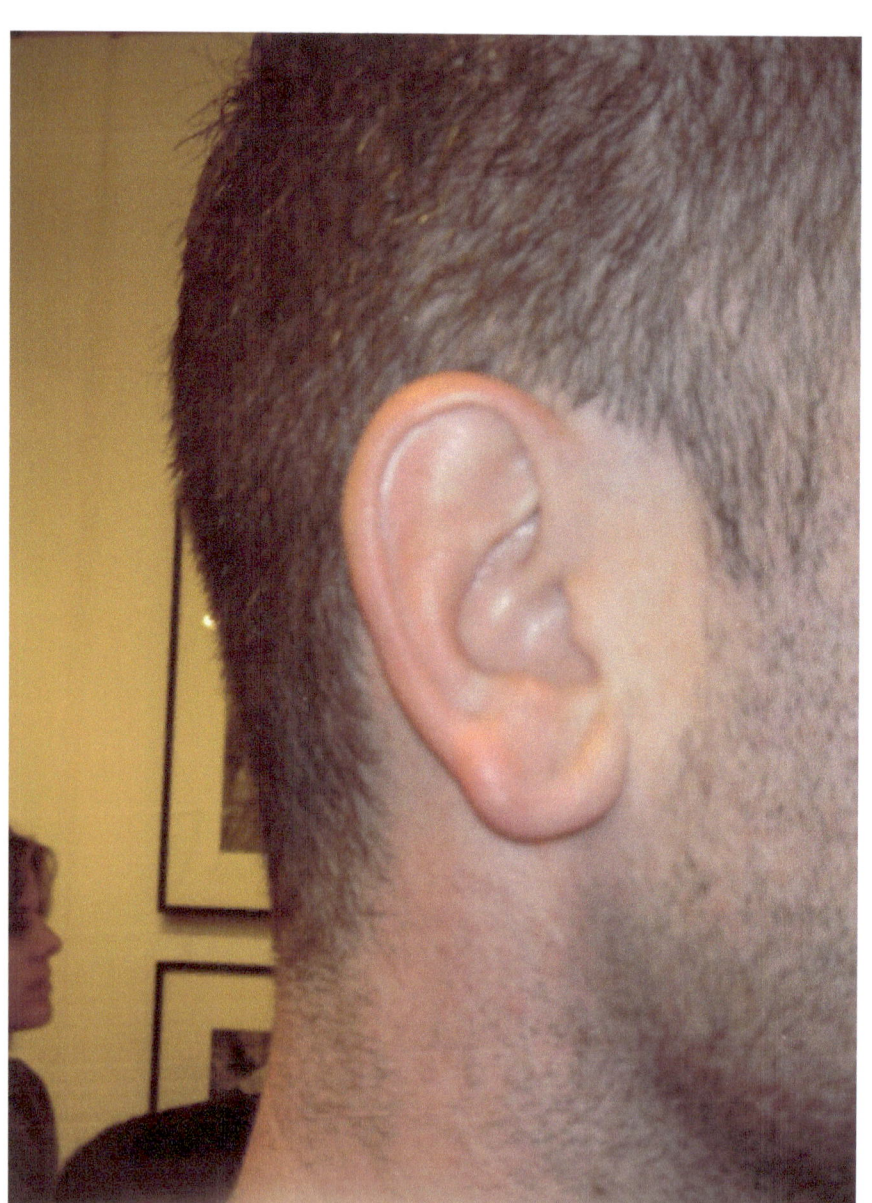

taste

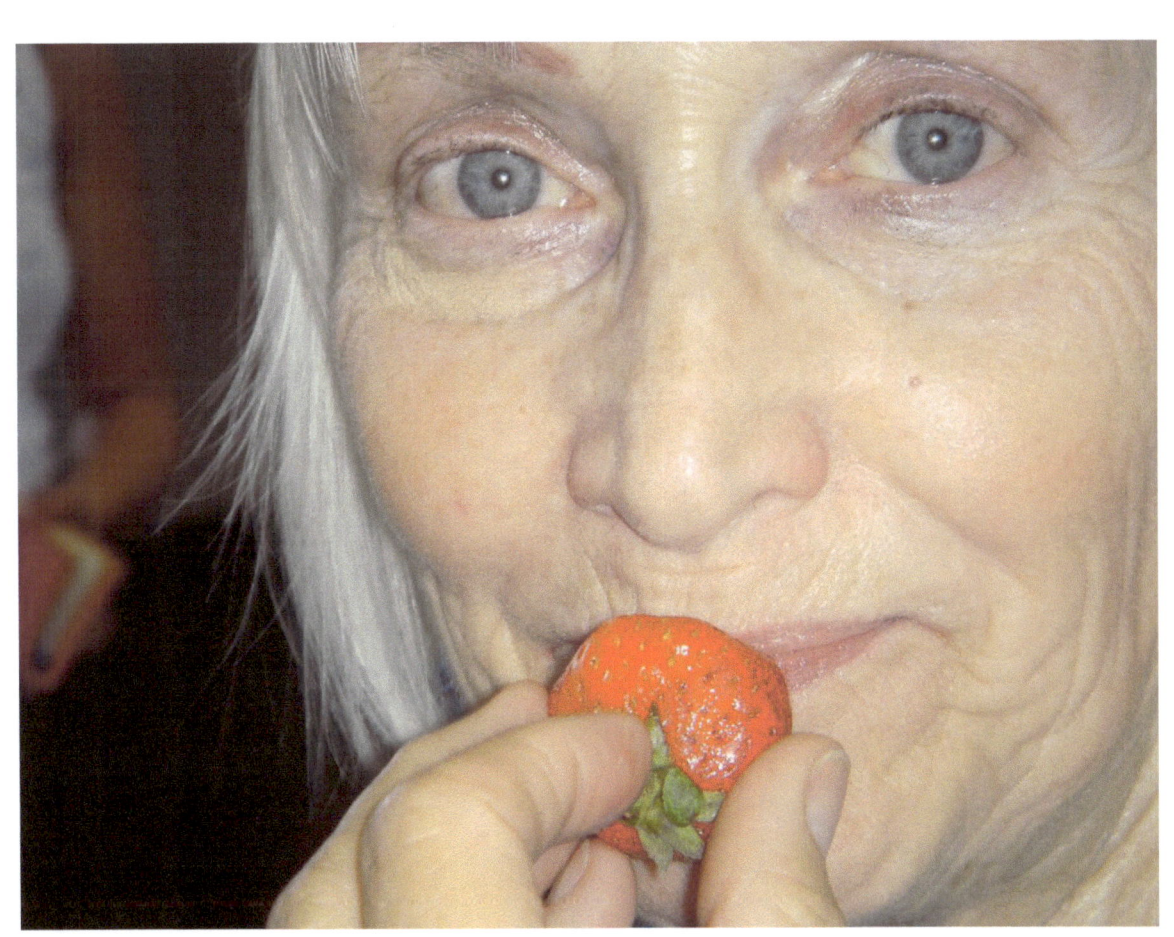

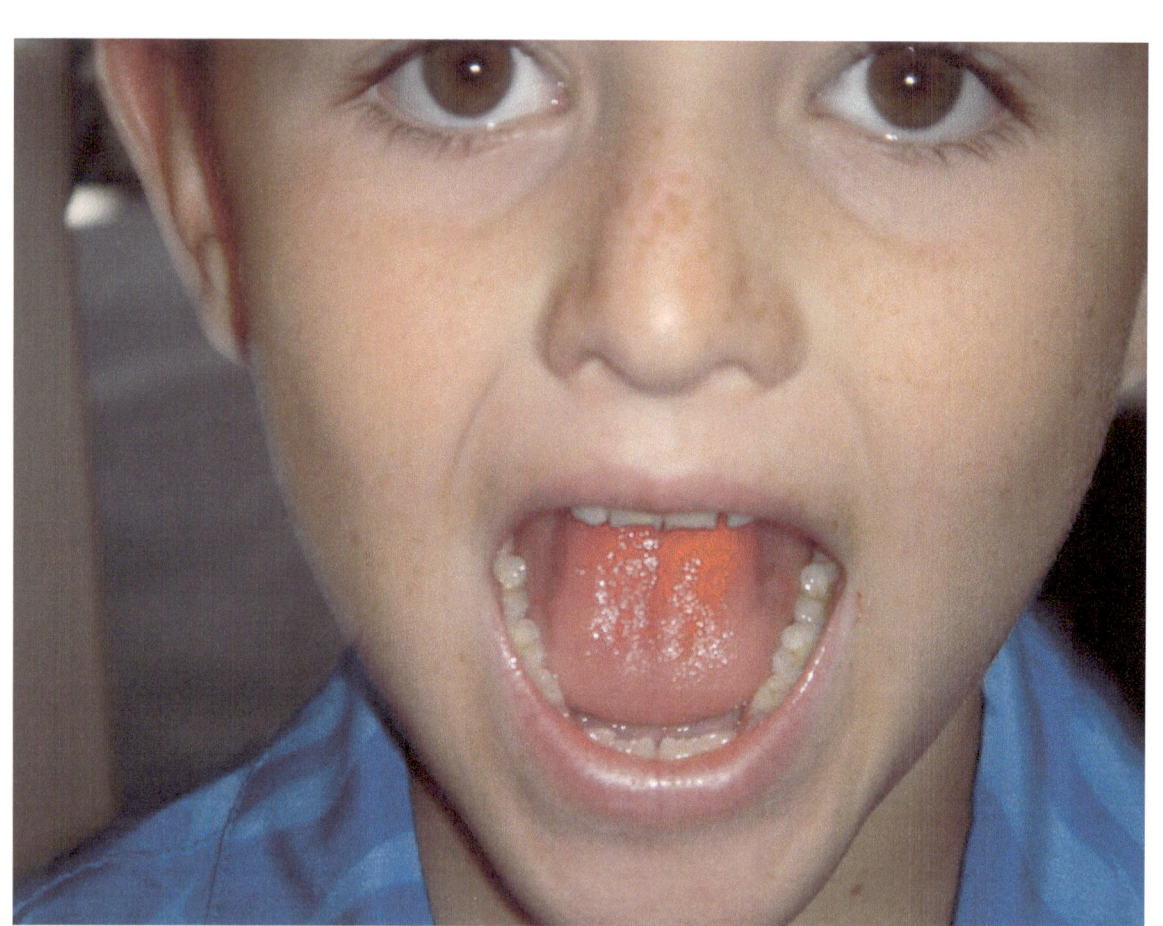

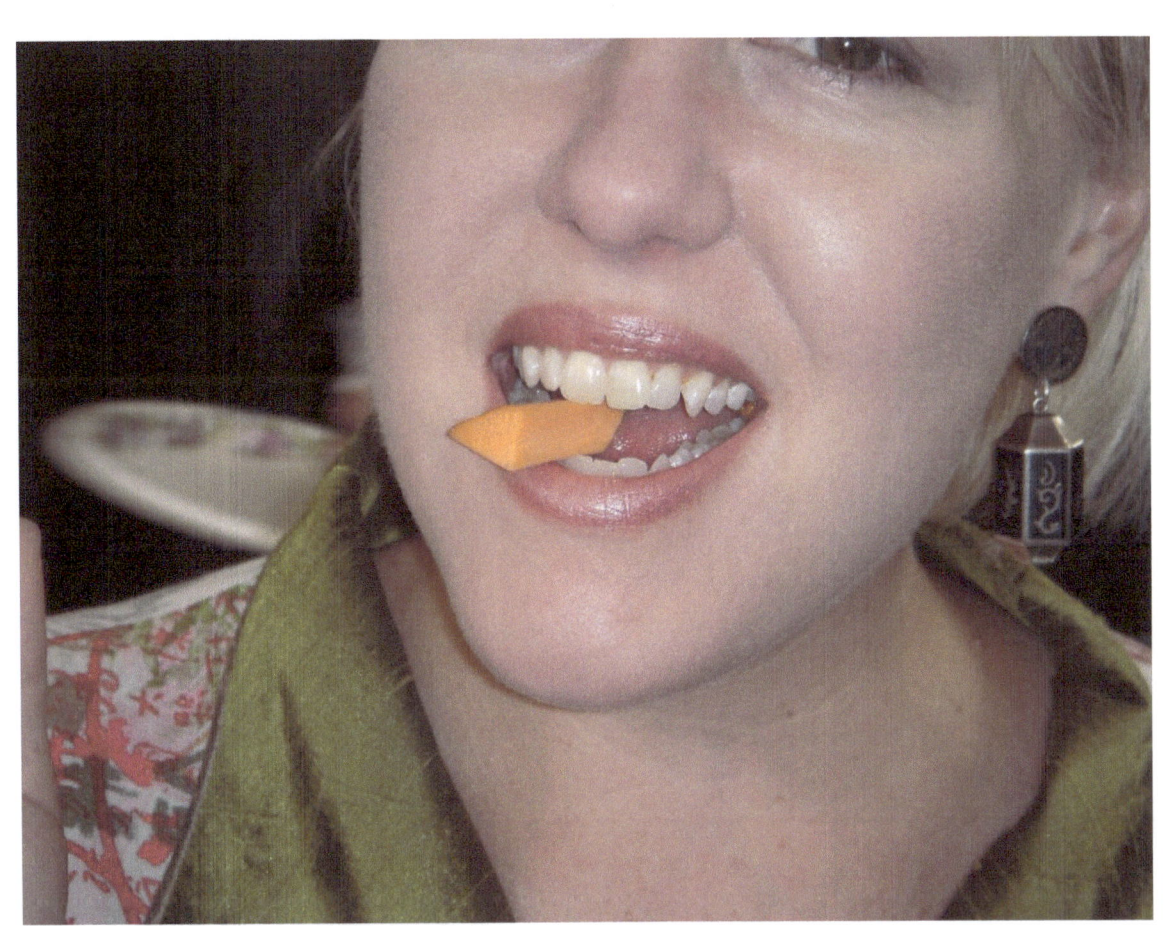

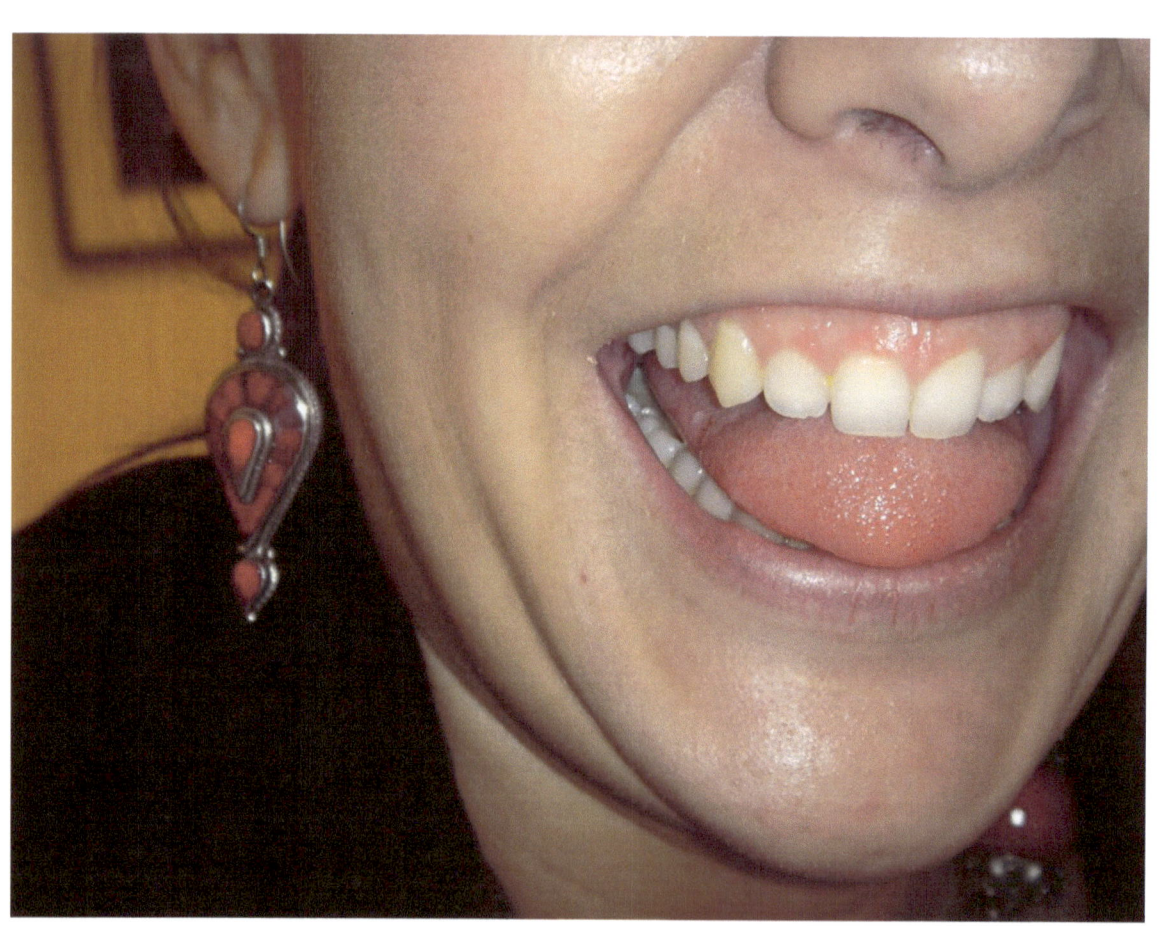

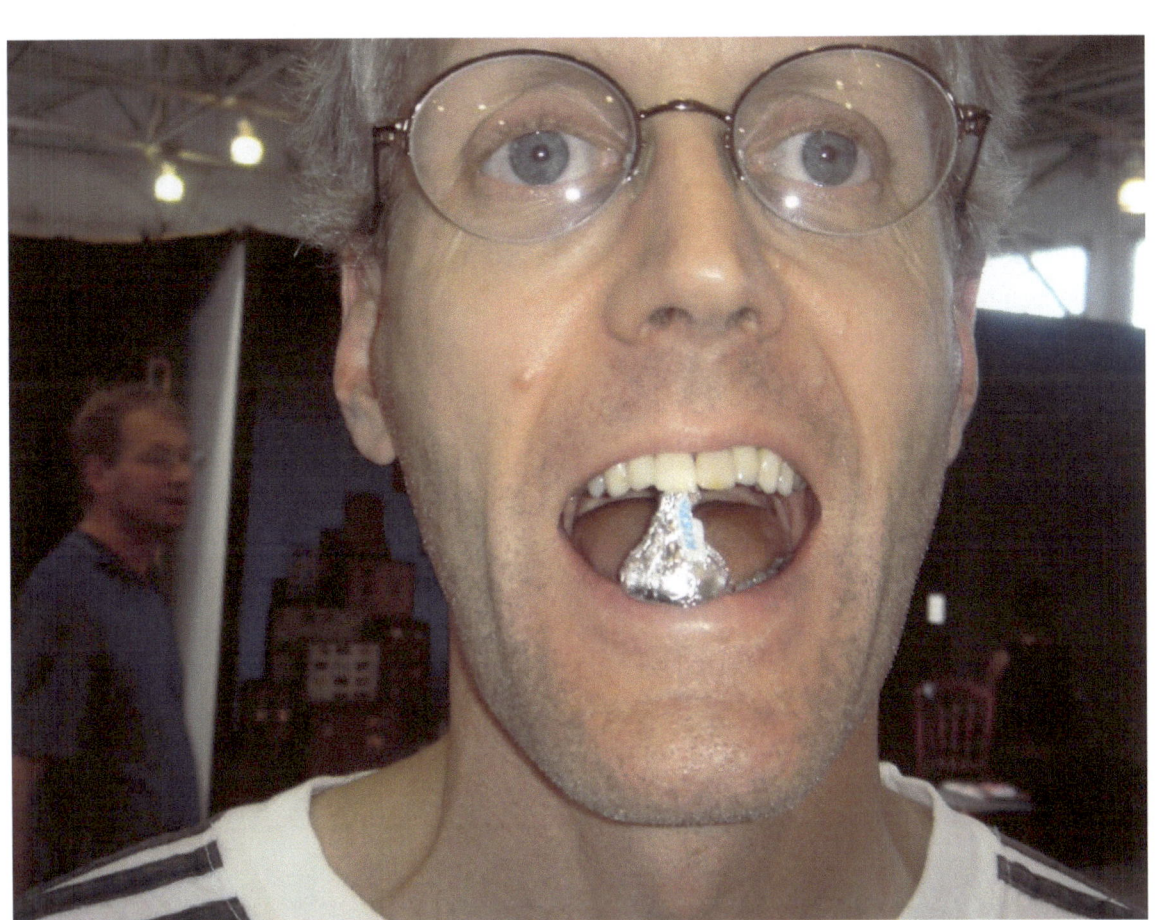

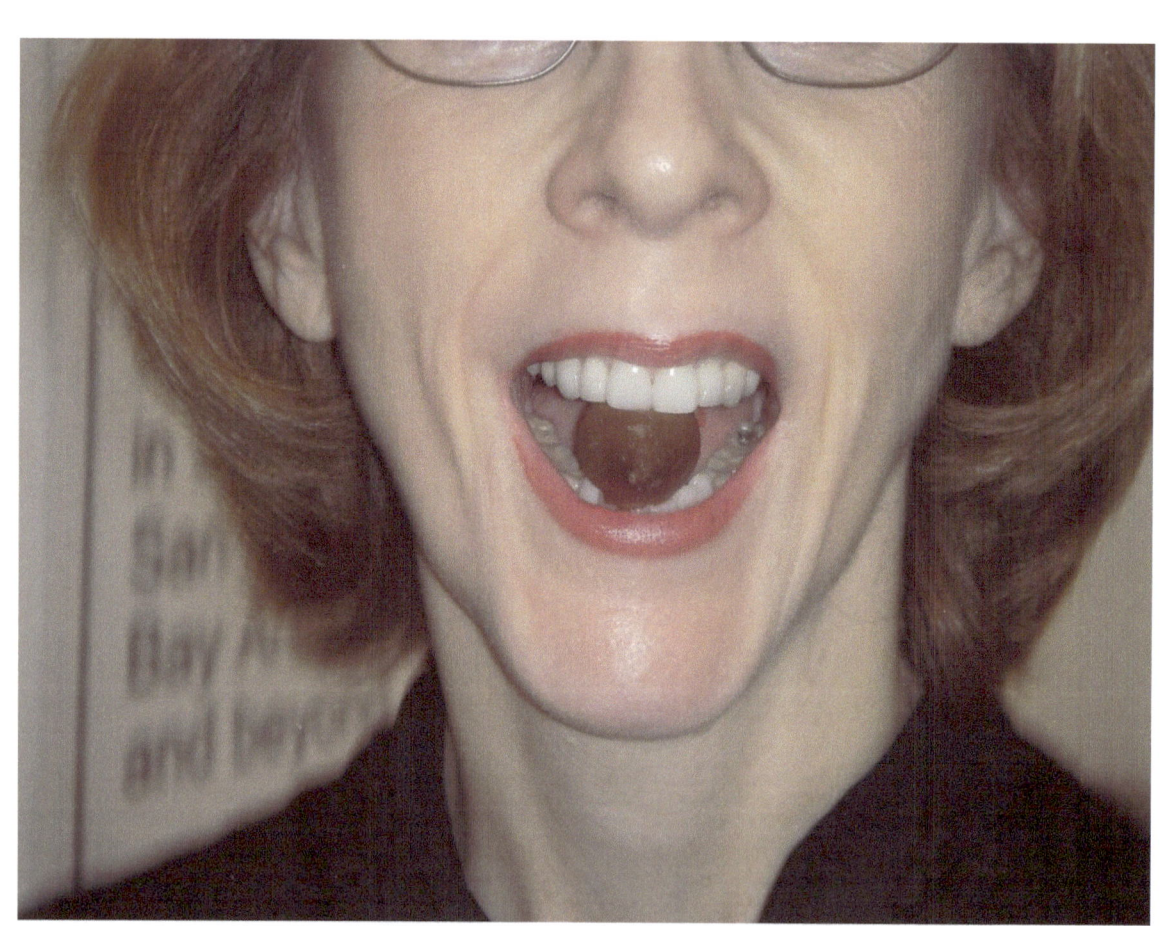

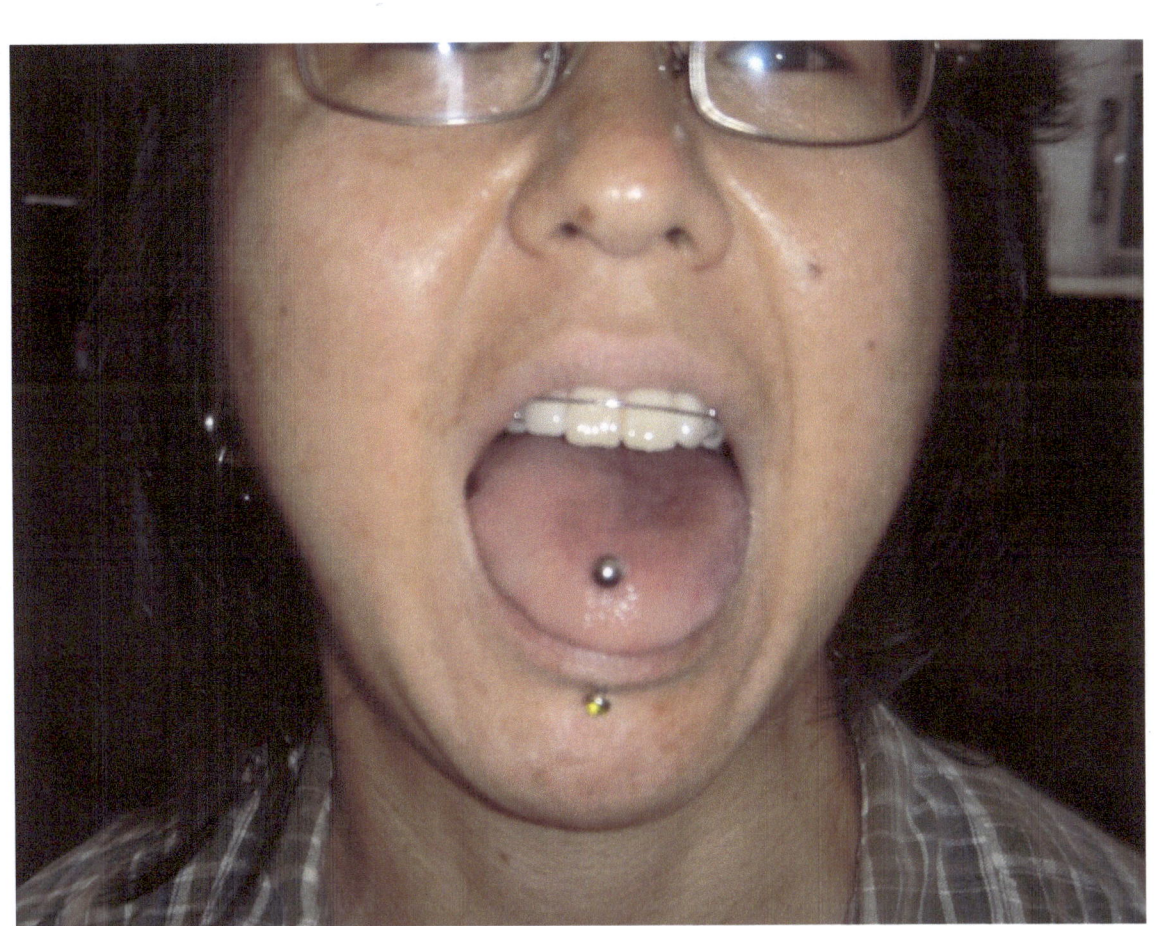

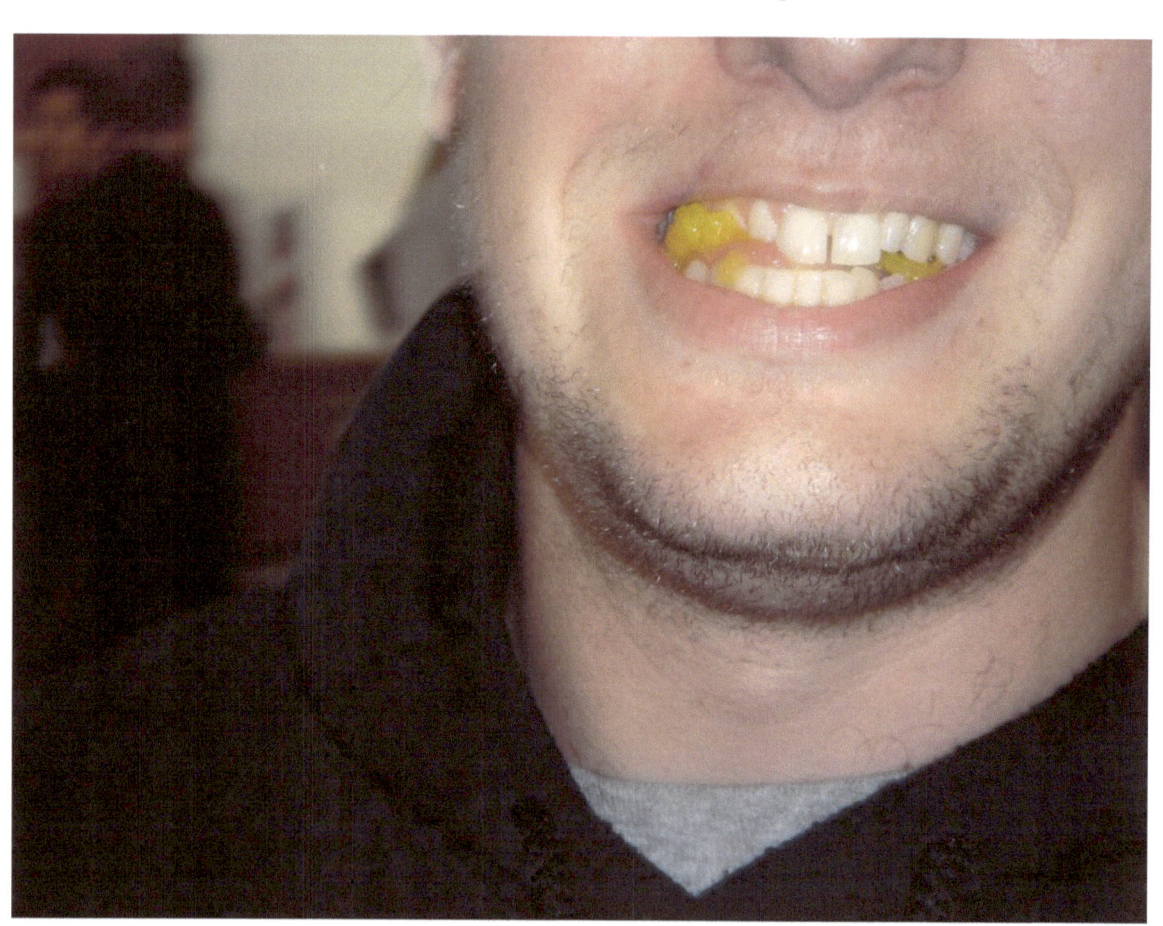

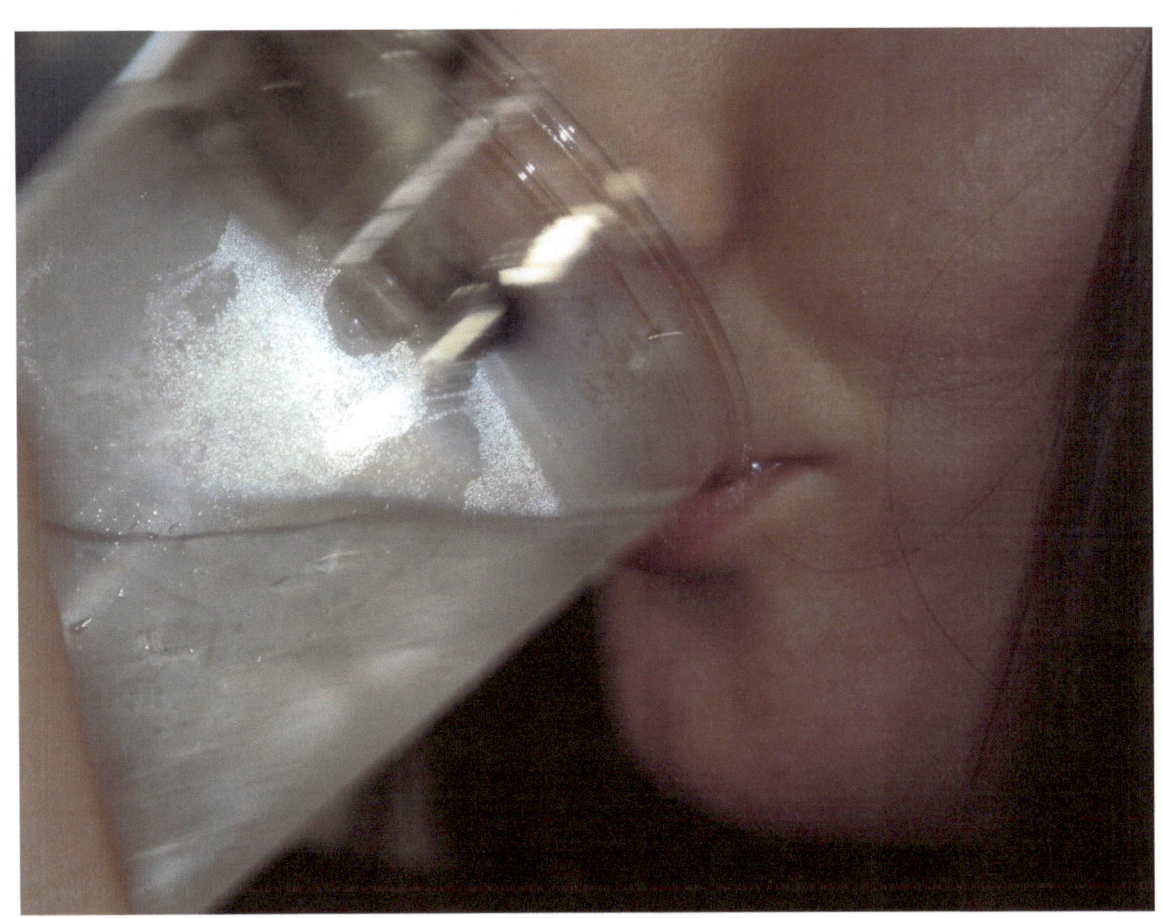

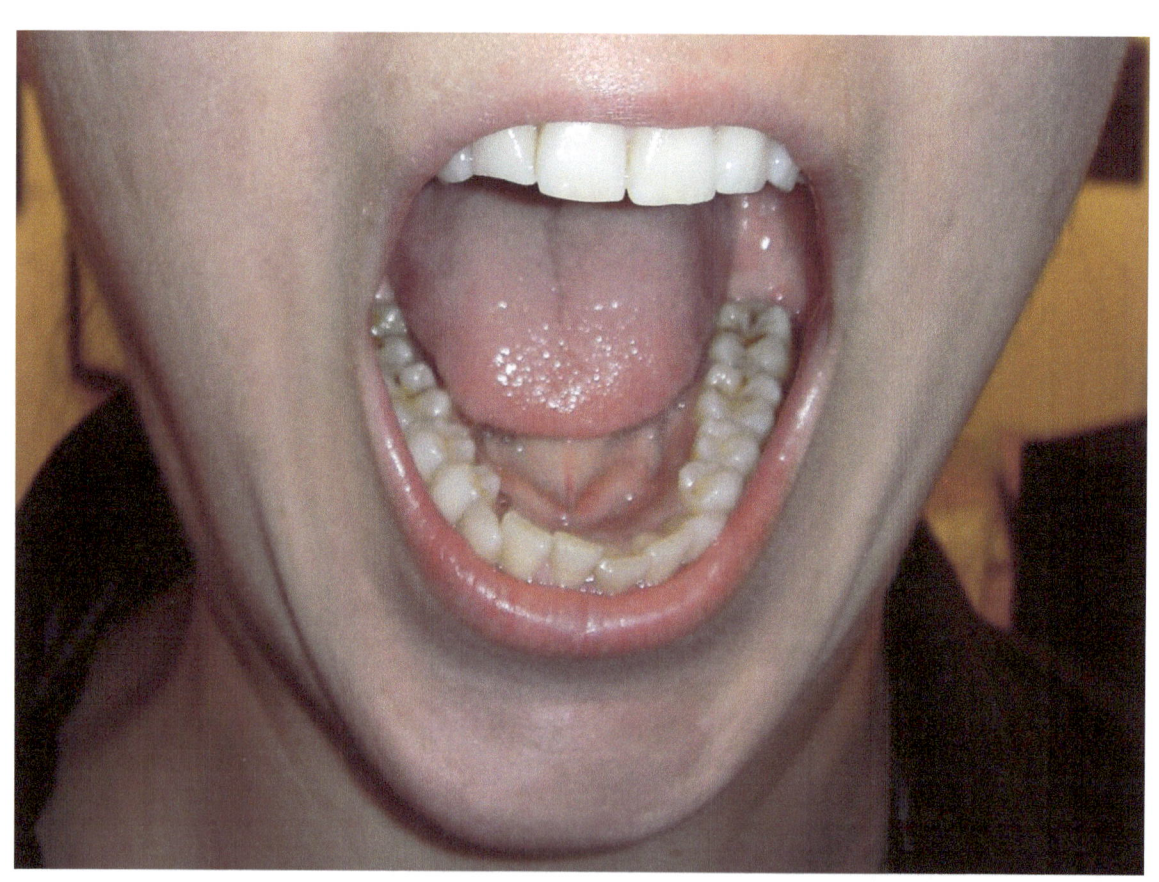

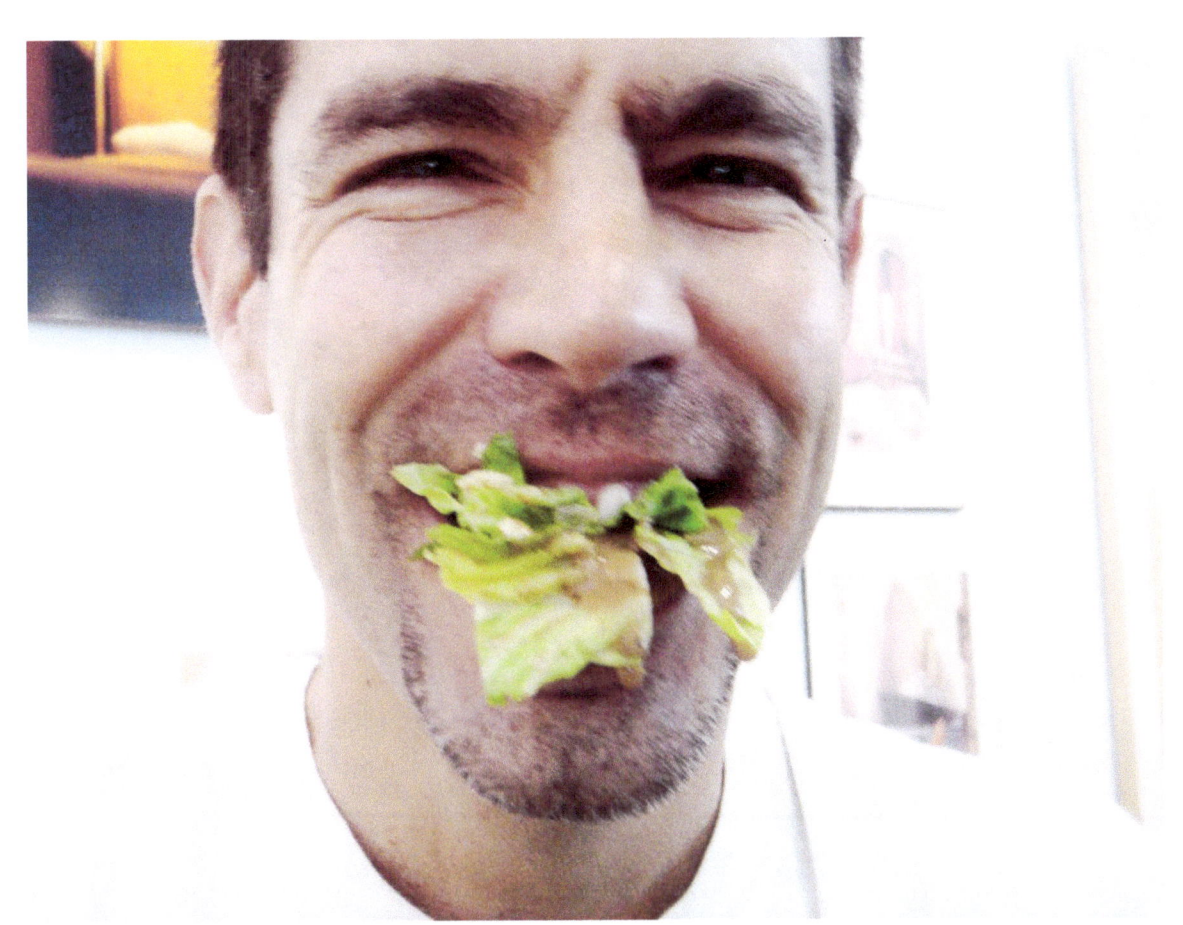

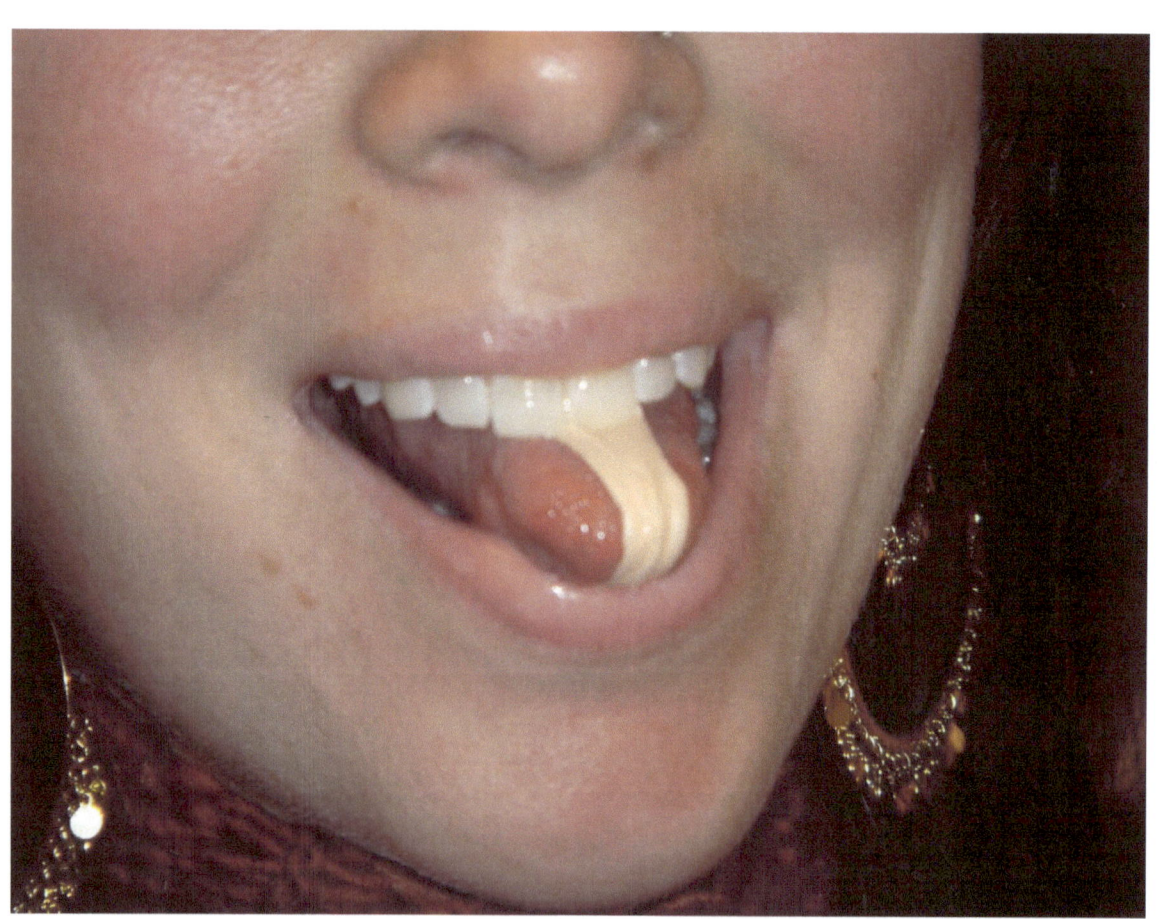

smell

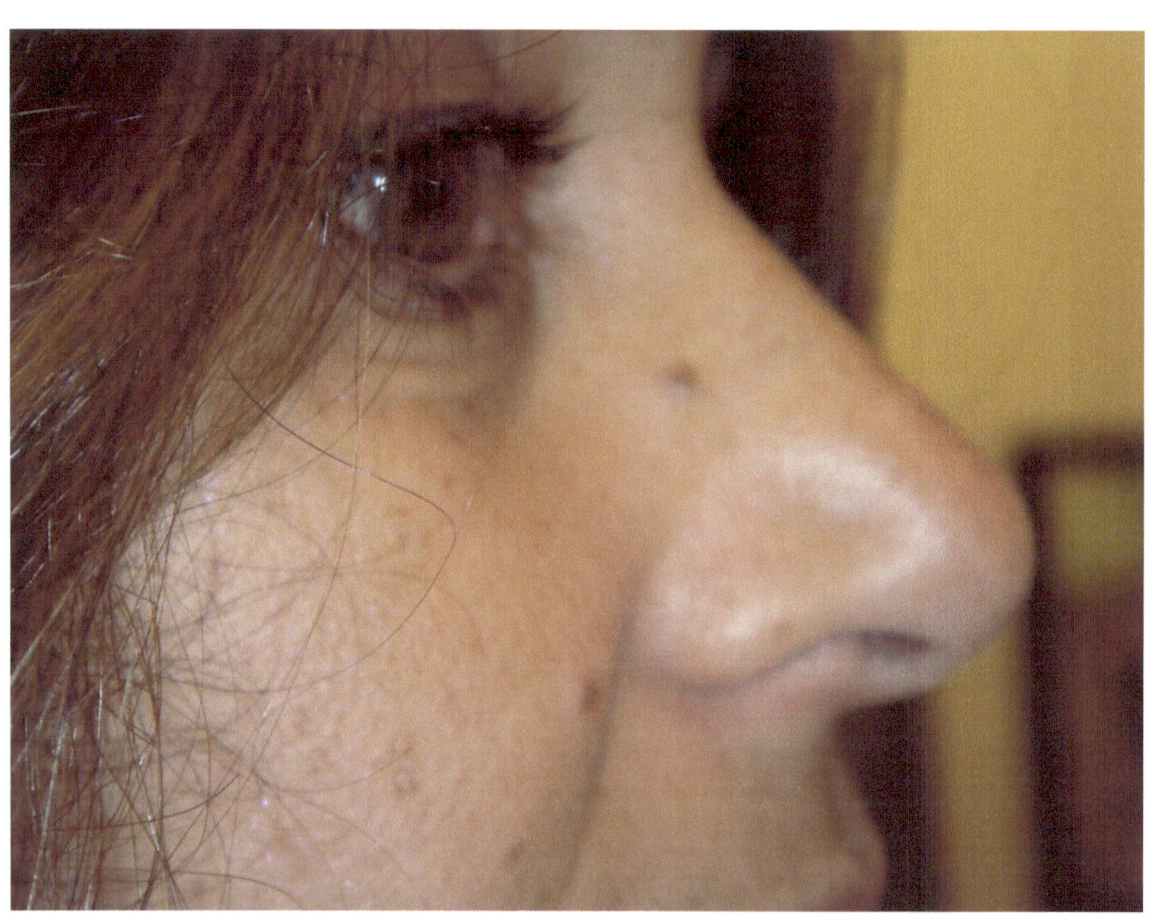

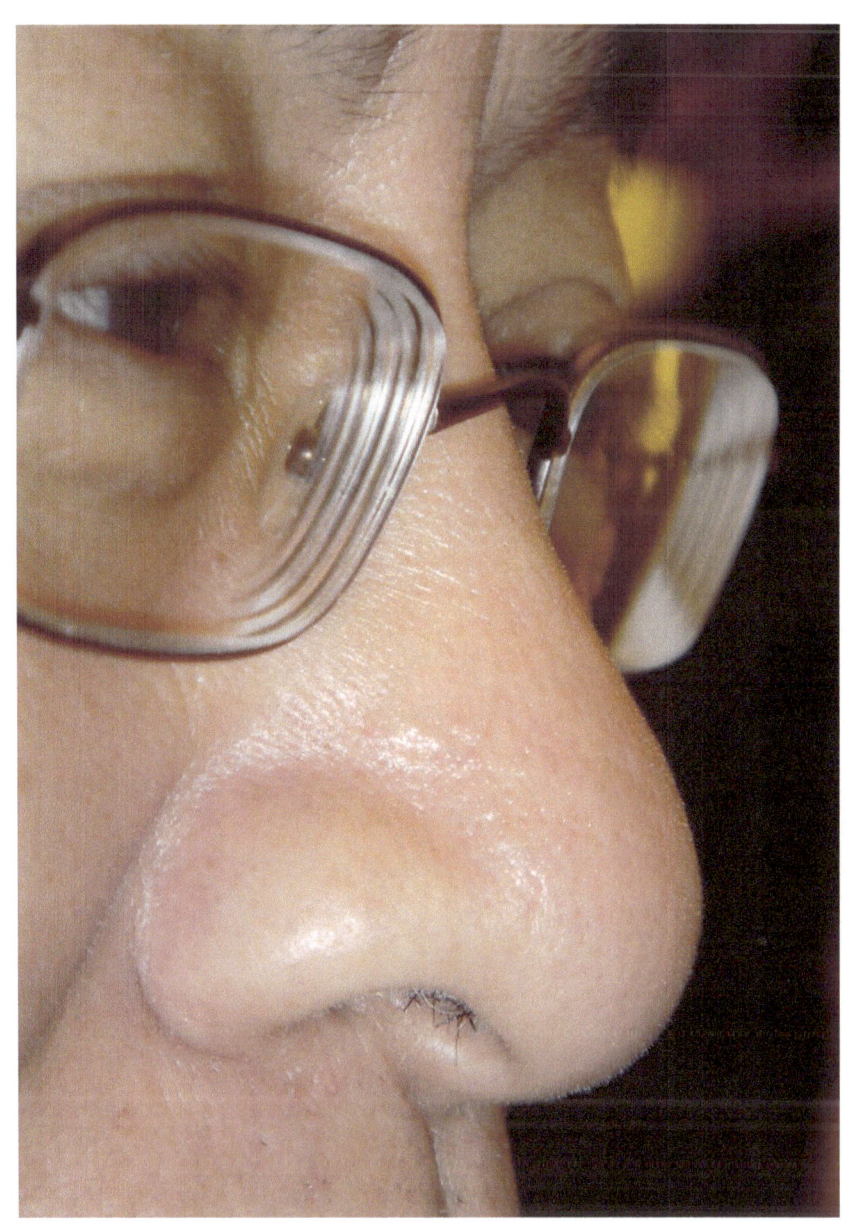

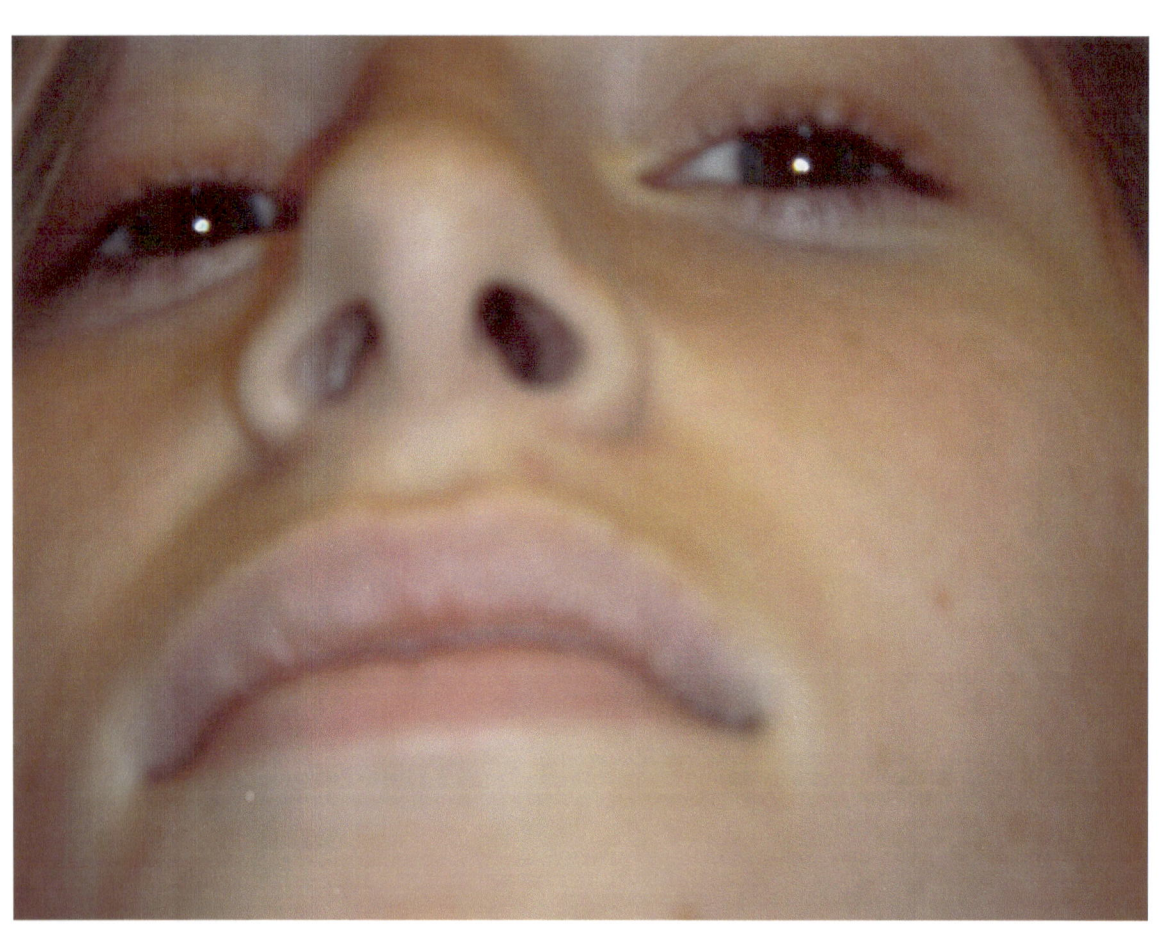

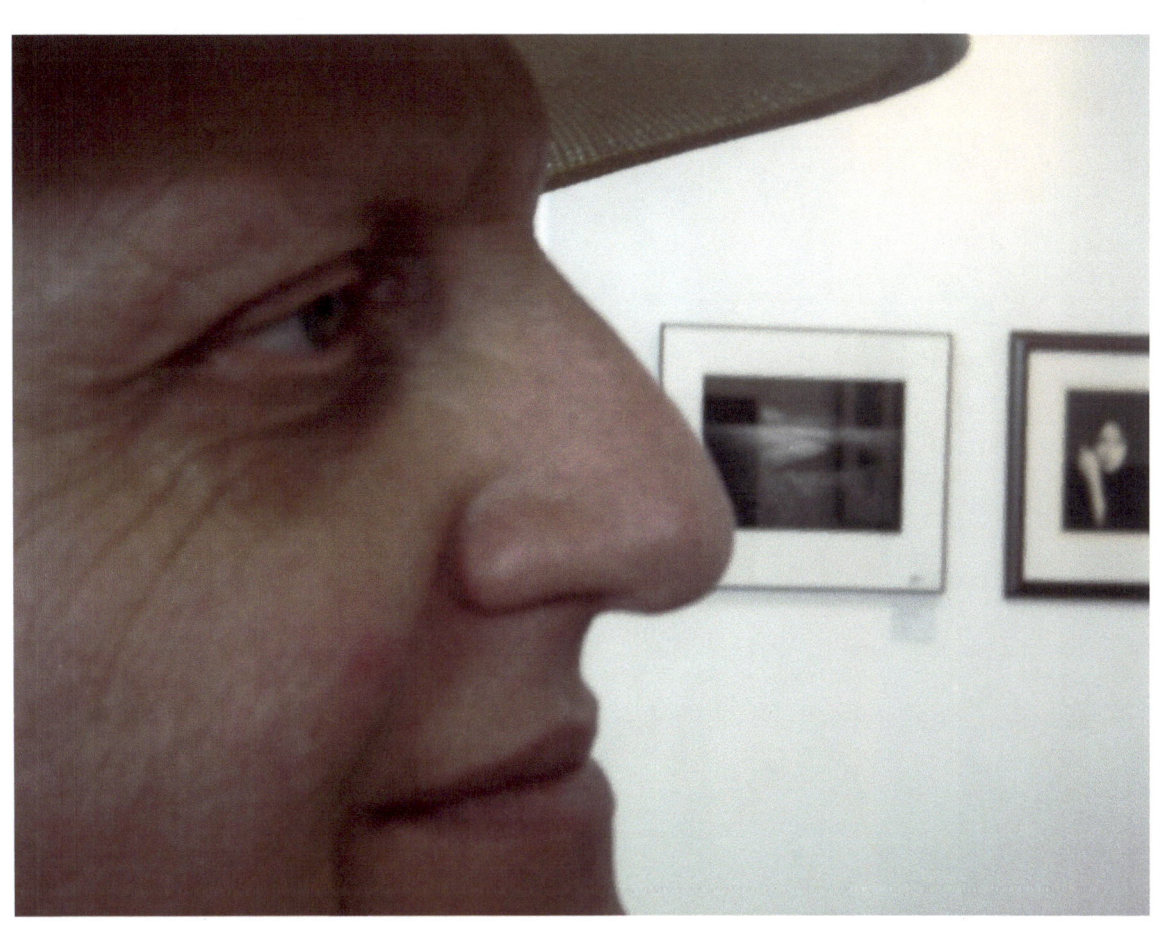

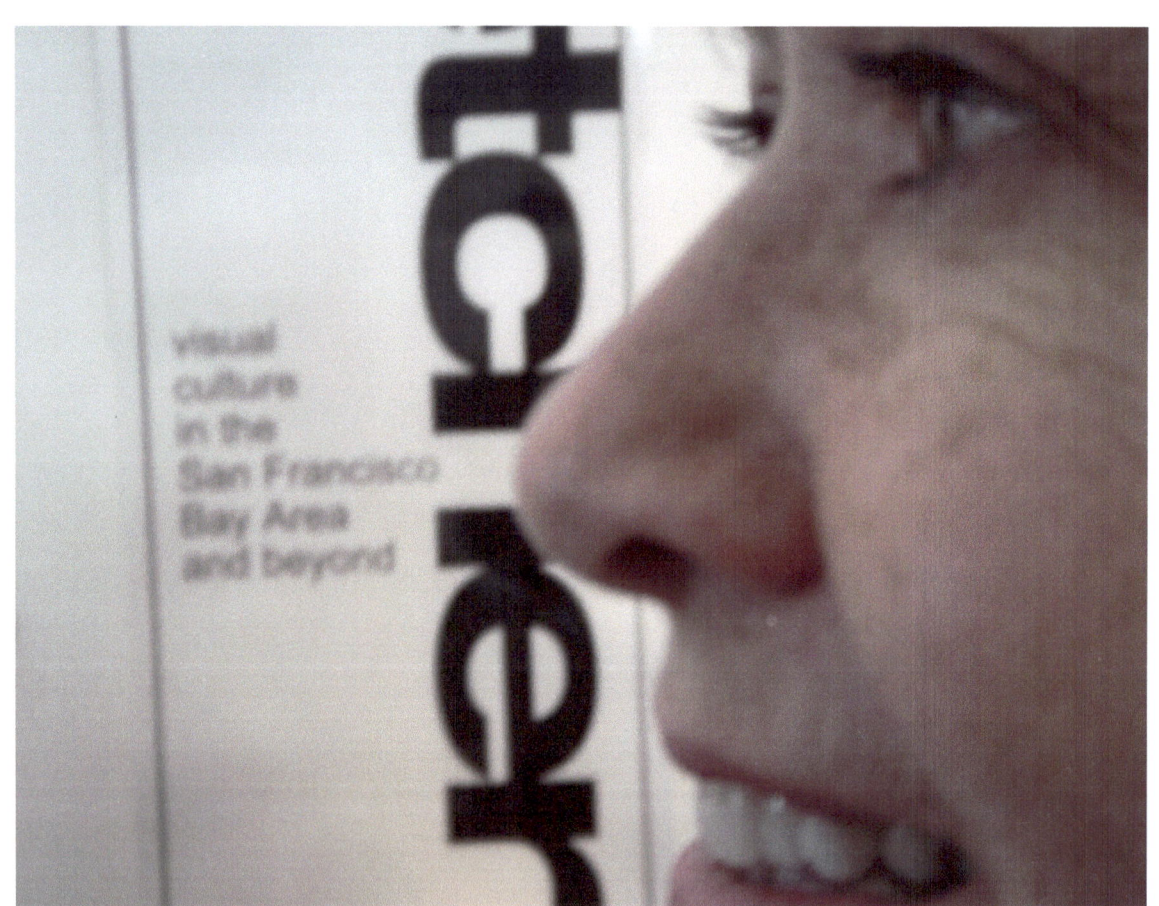

visual
culture
in the
San Francisco
Bay Area
and beyond

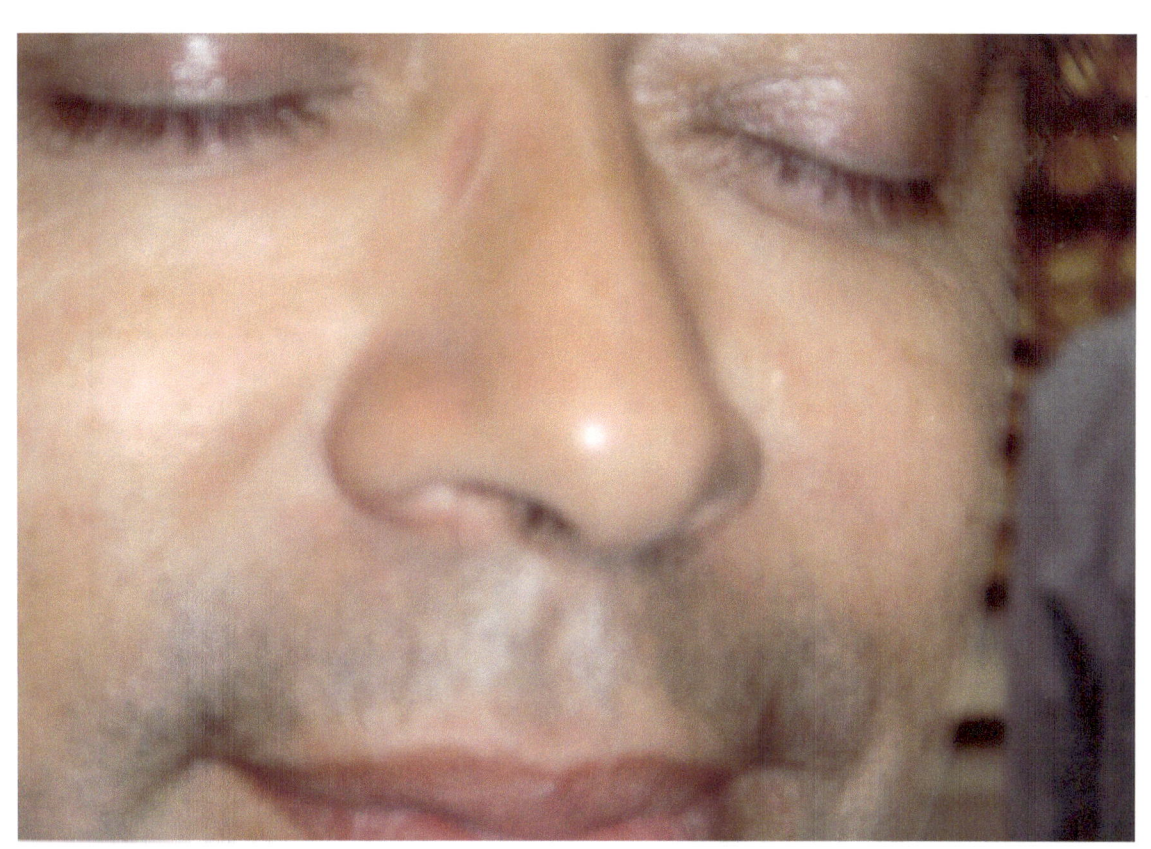

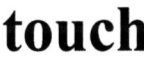

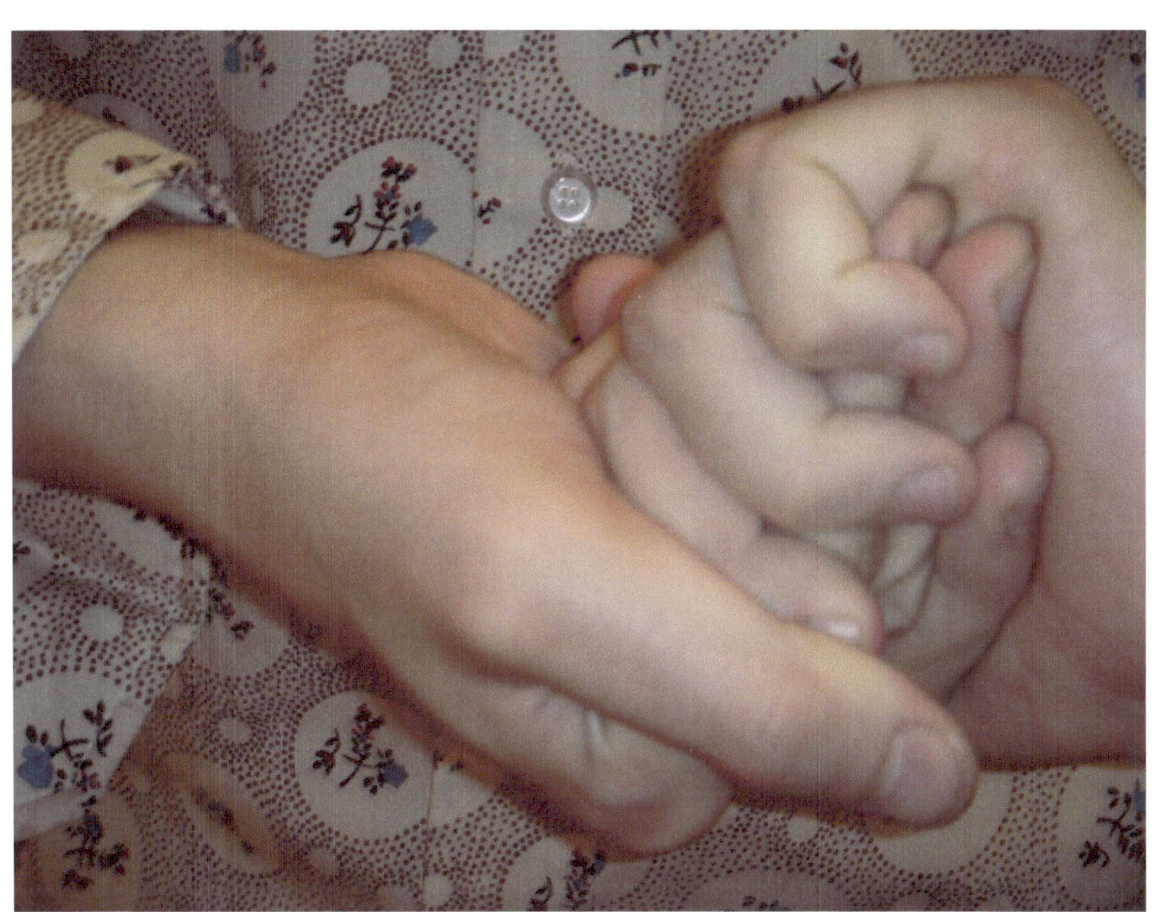

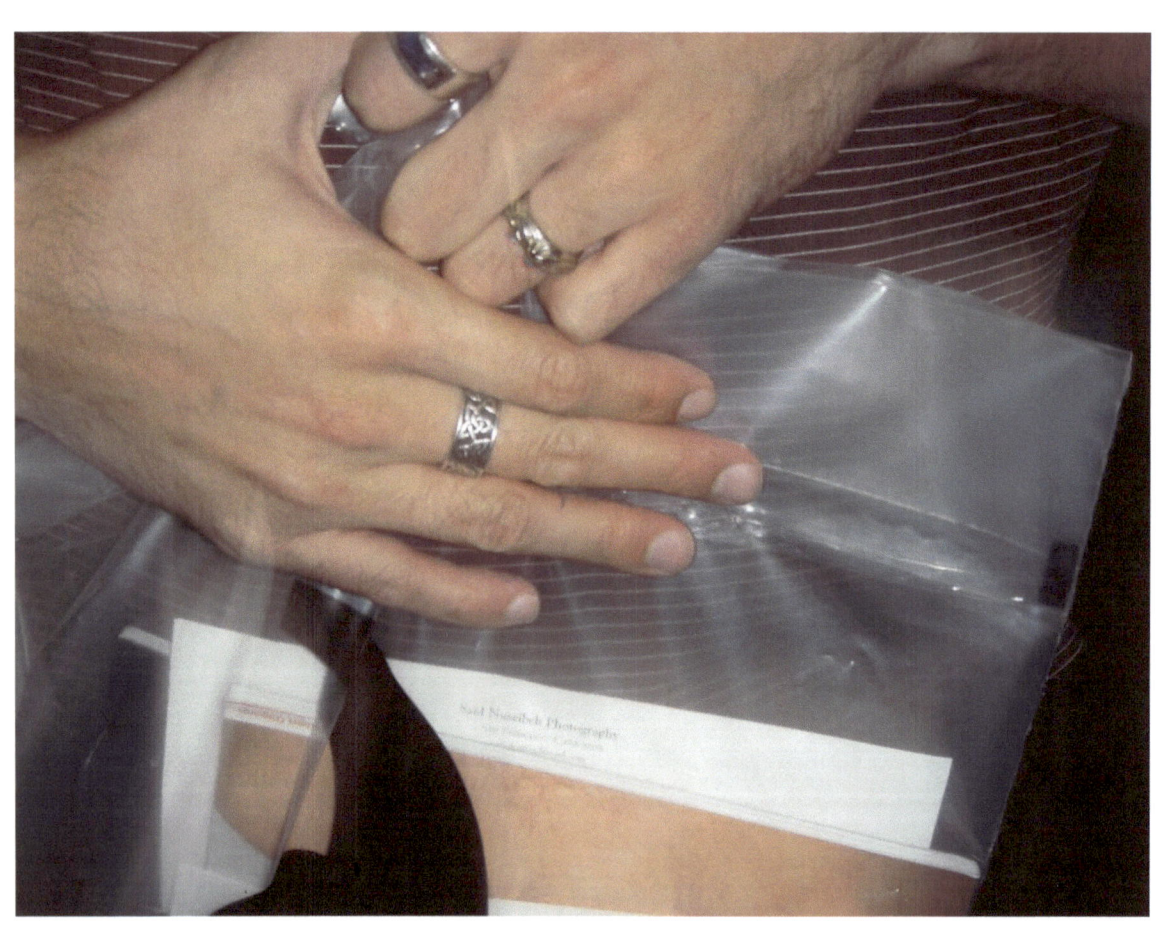

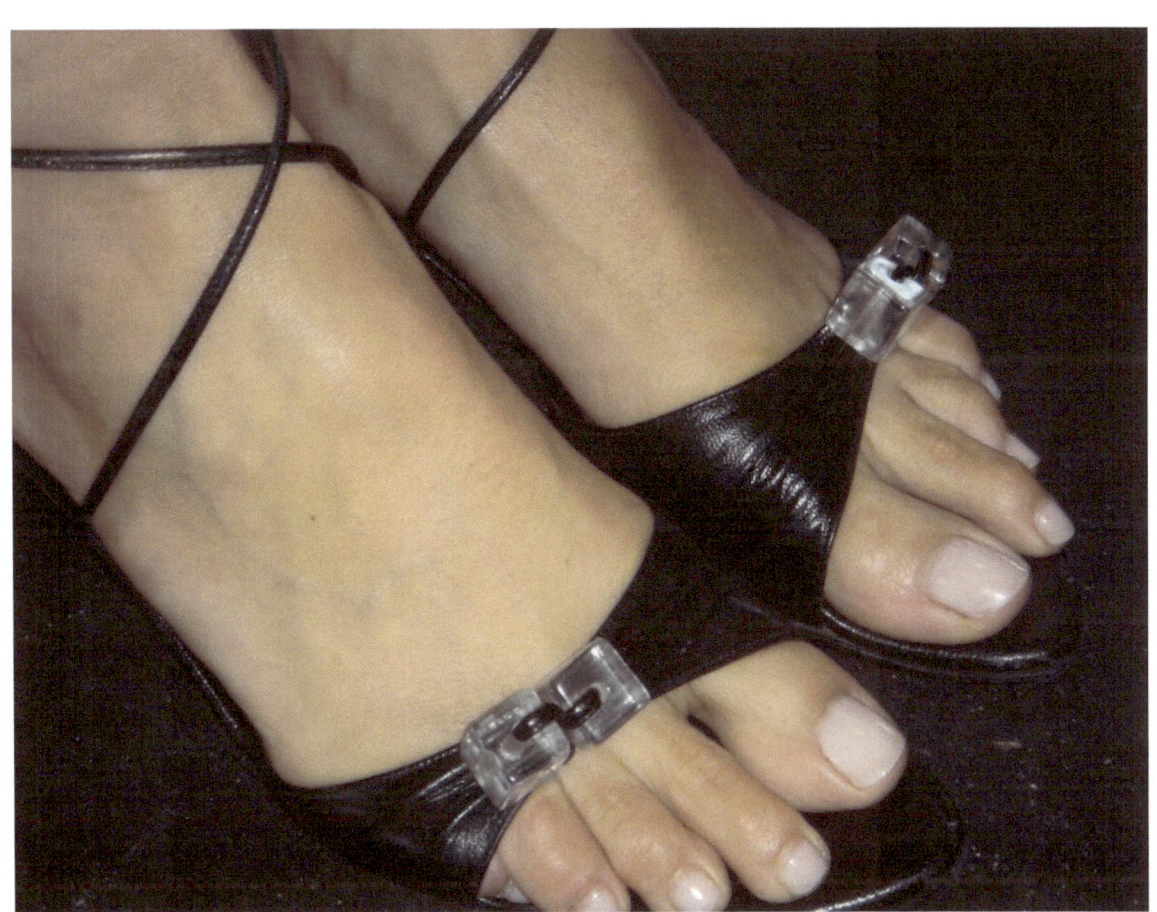

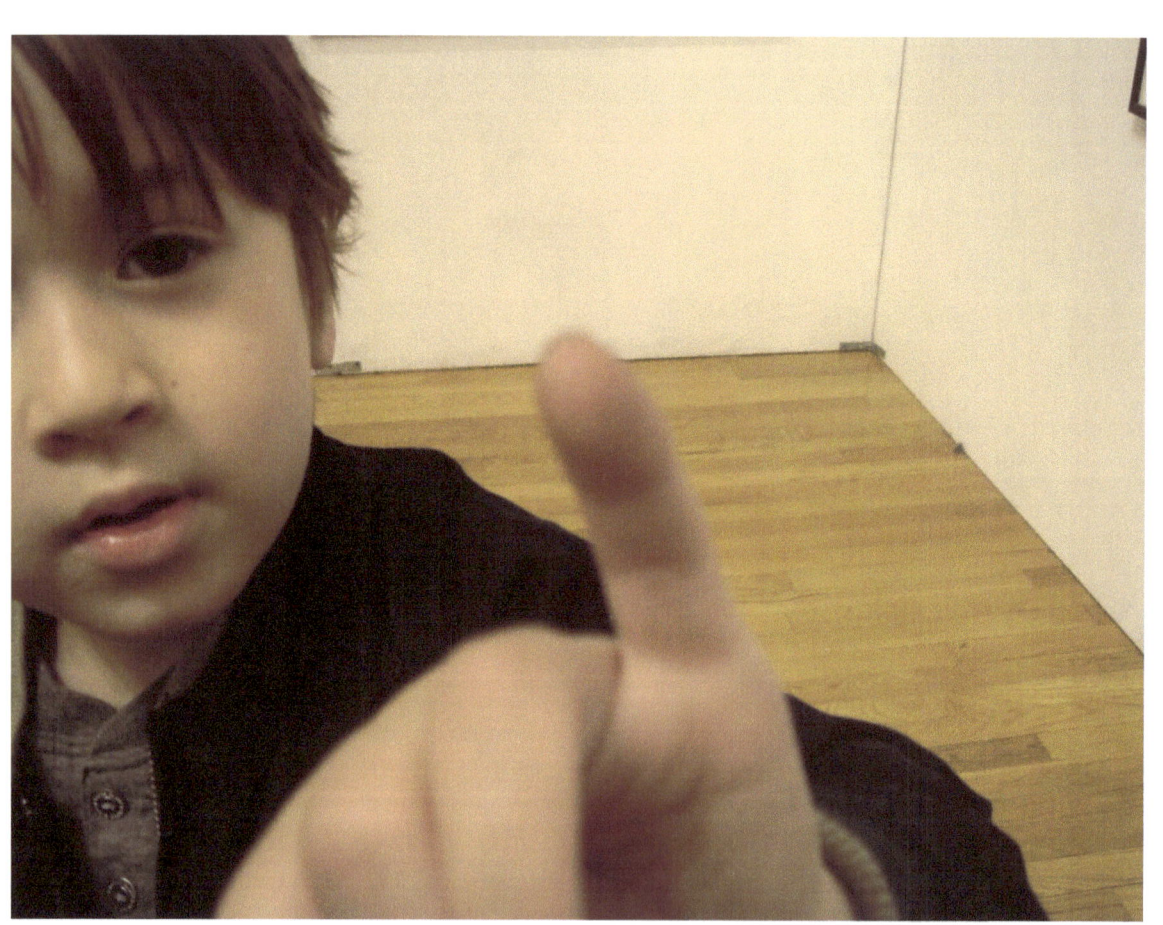

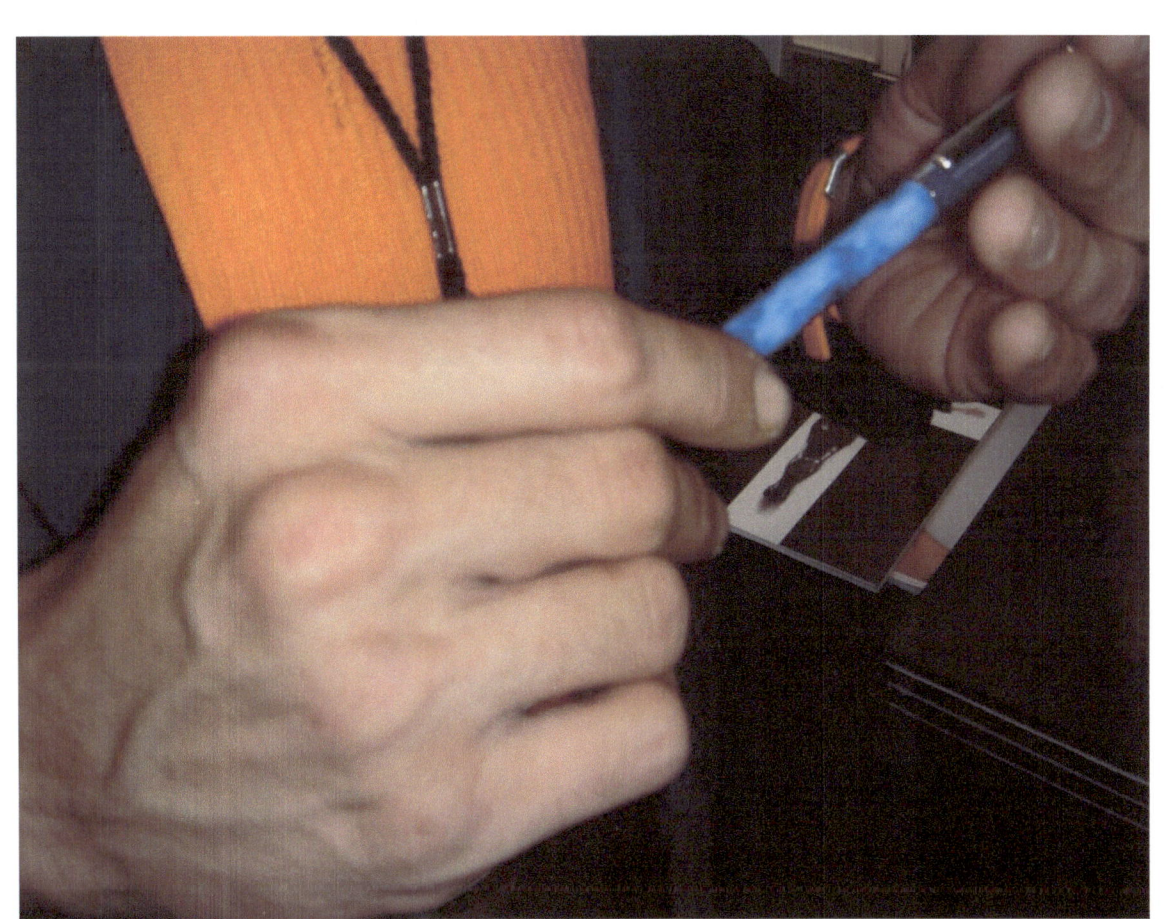

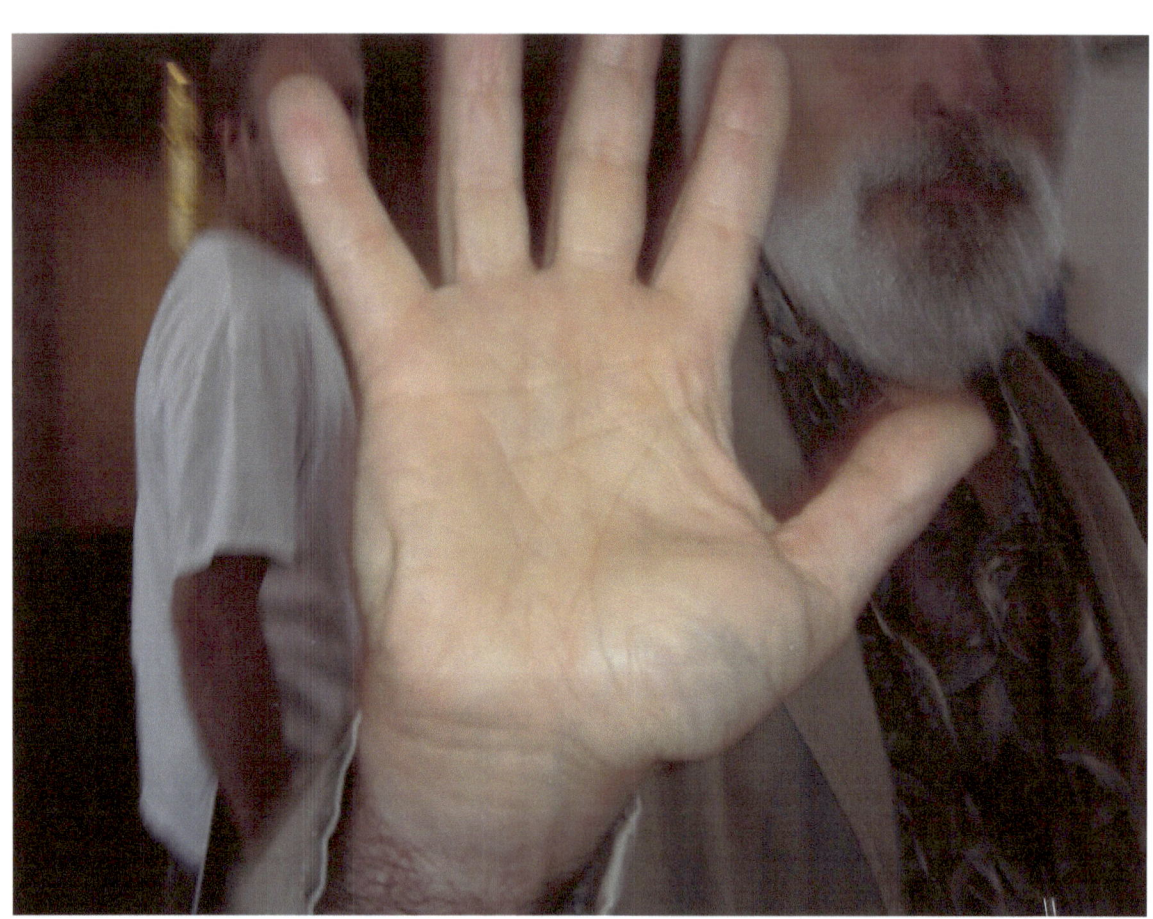

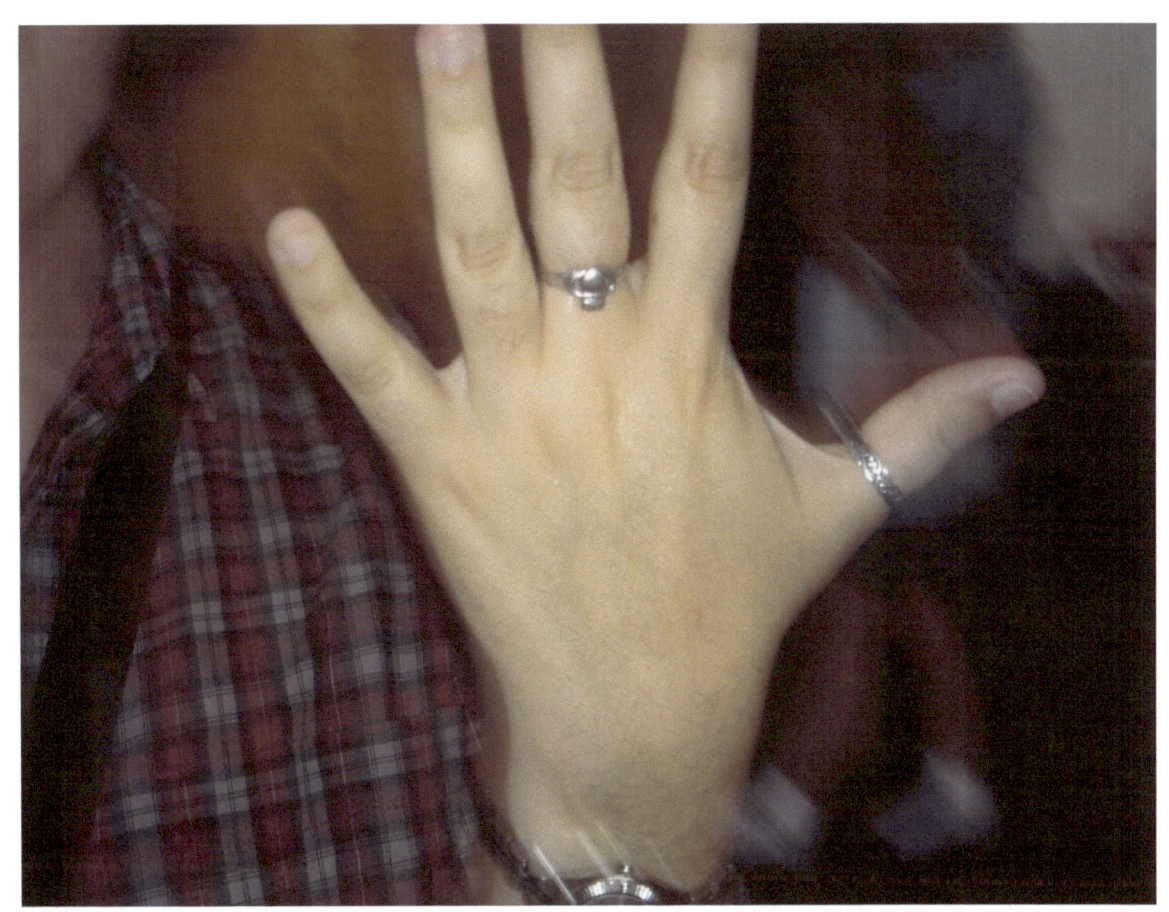

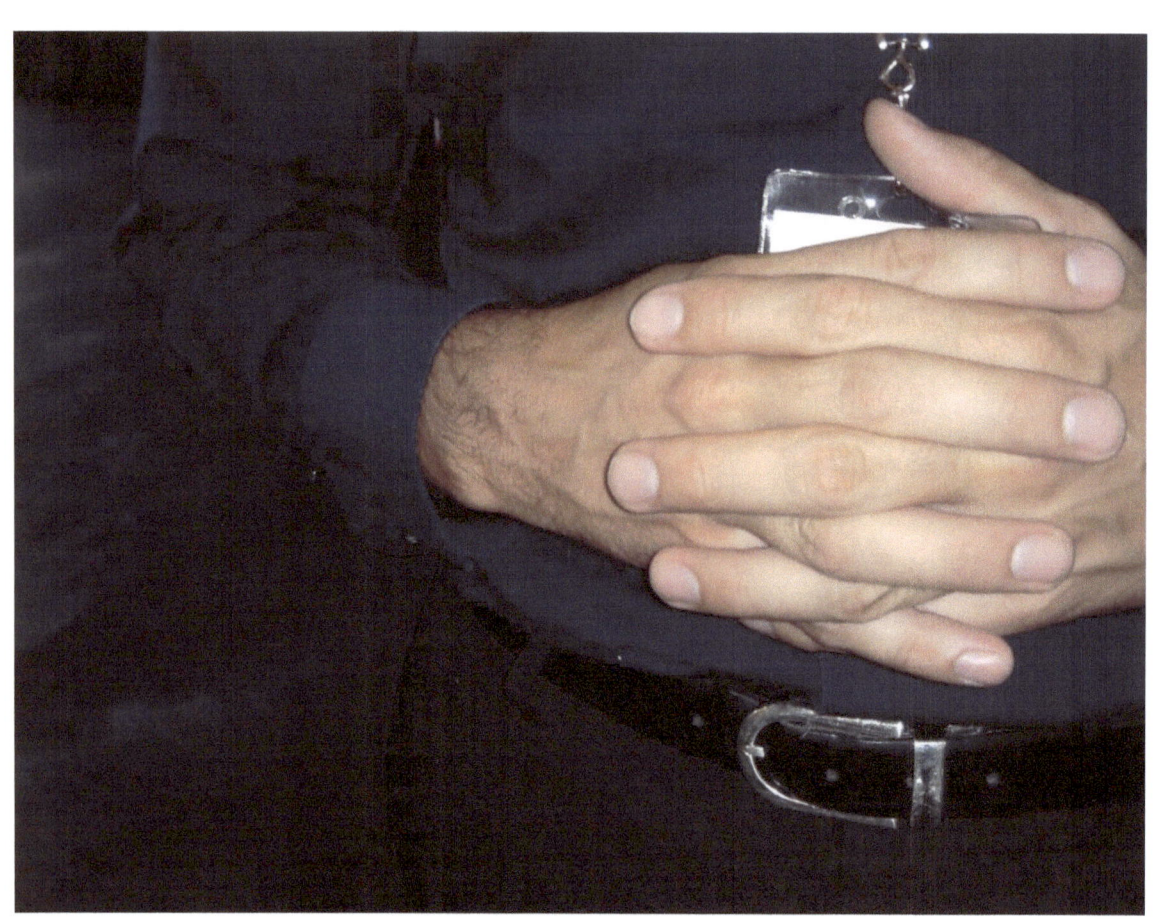

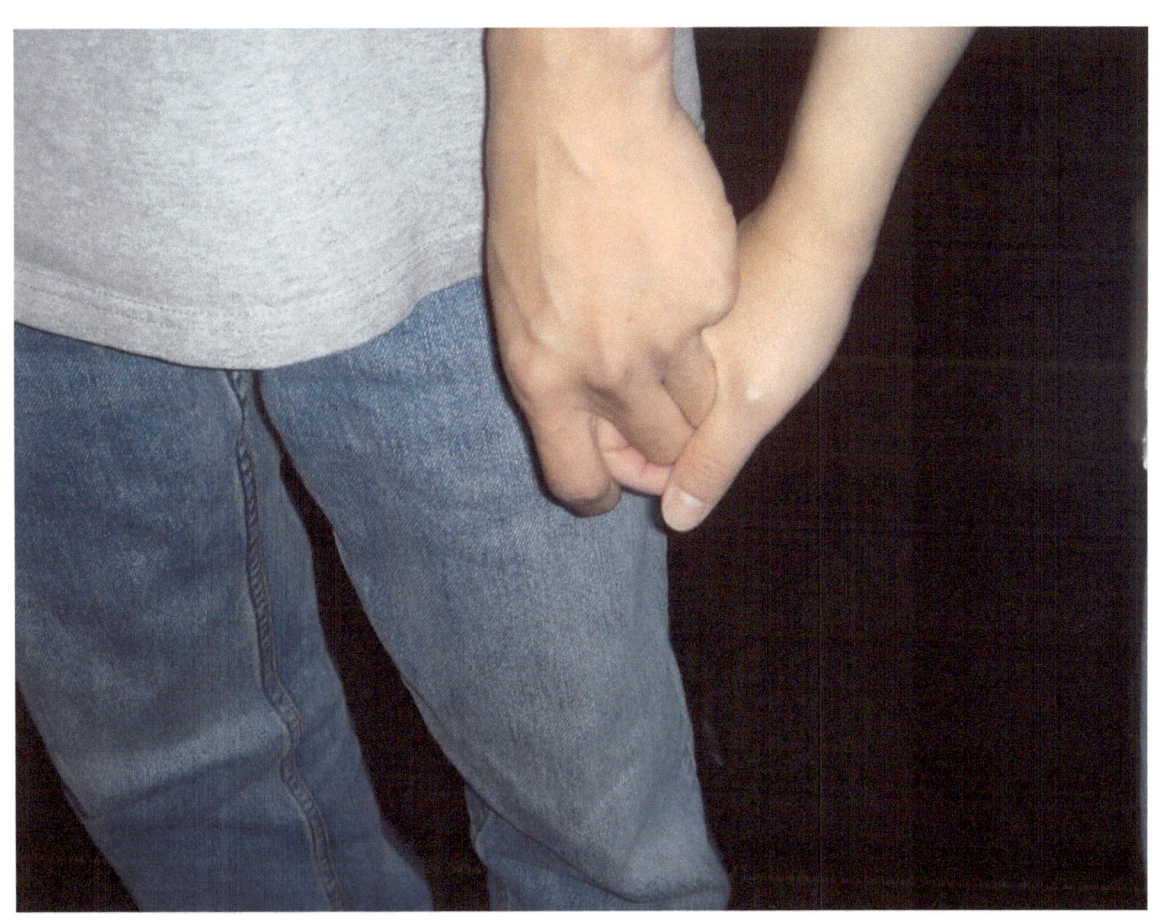

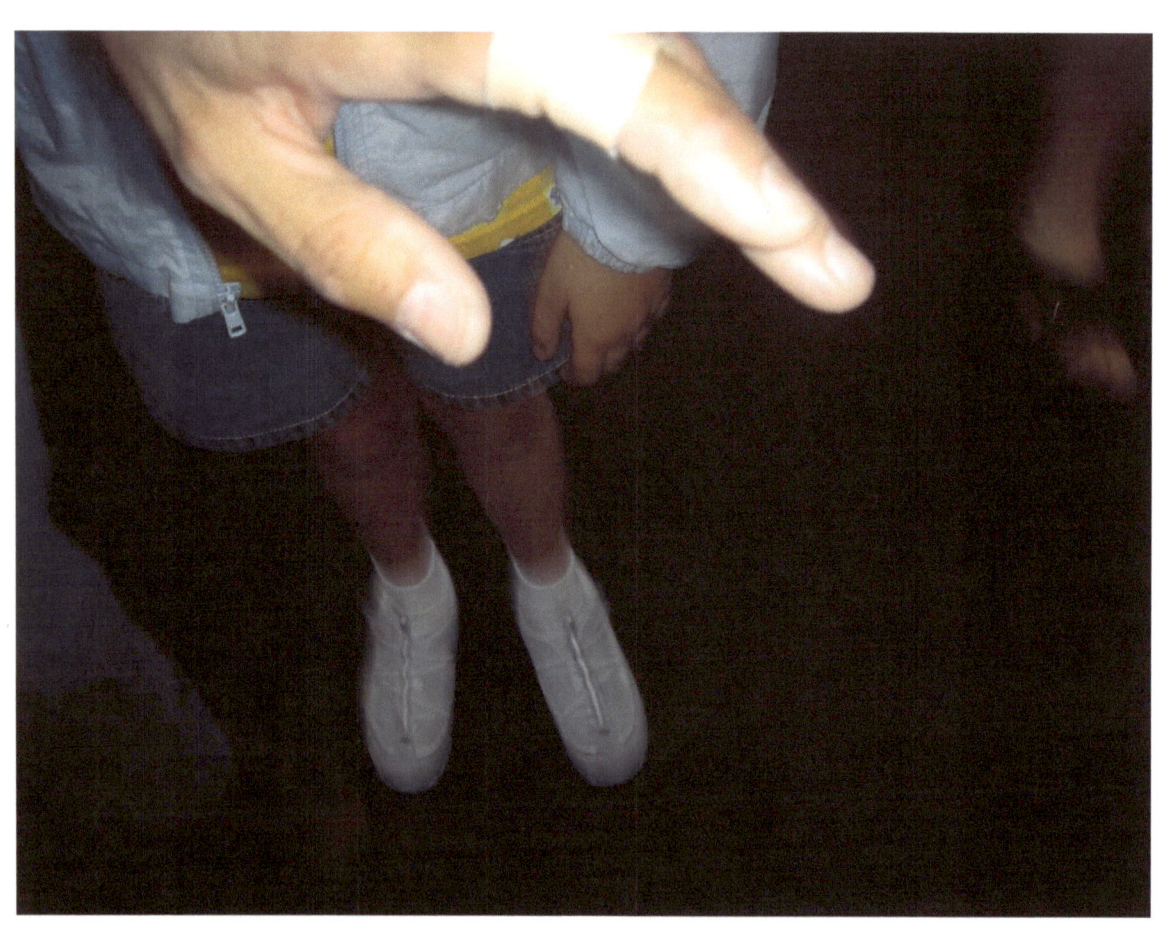

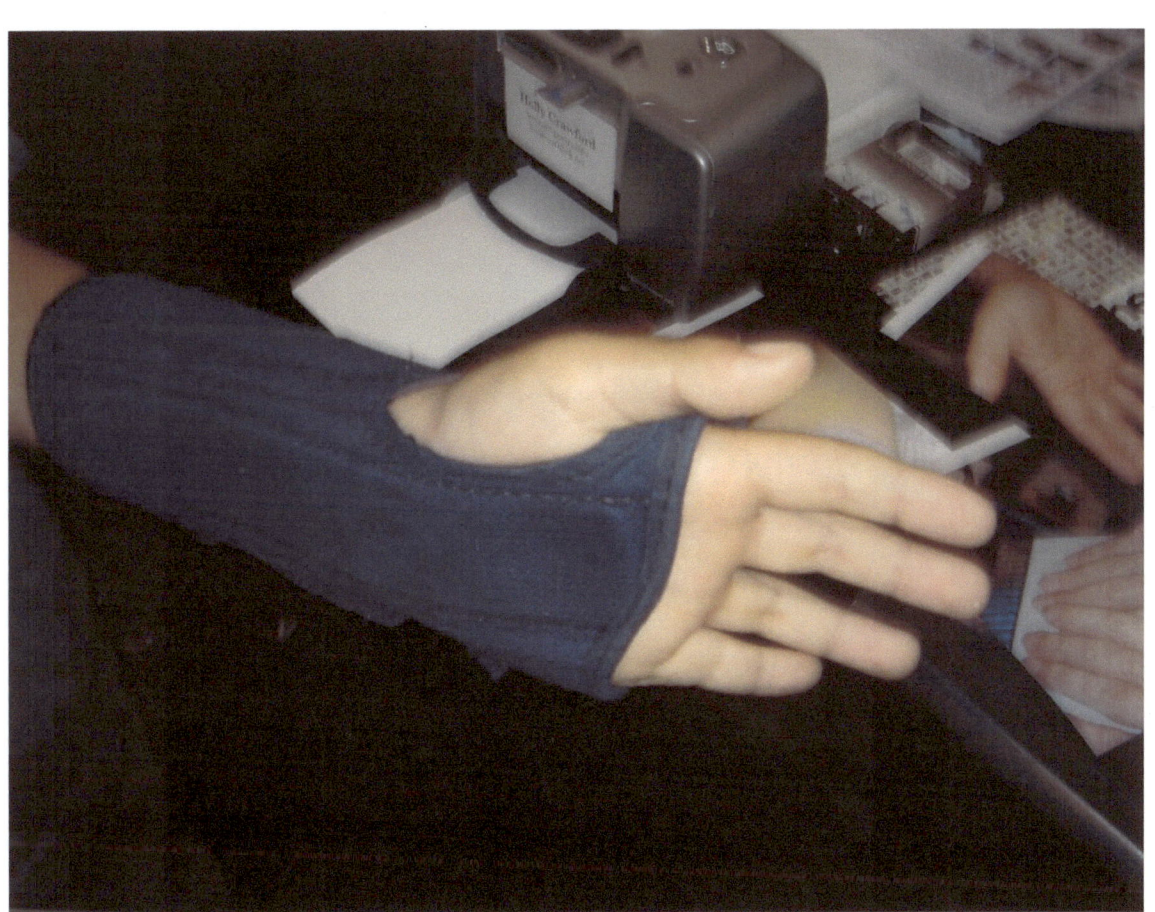

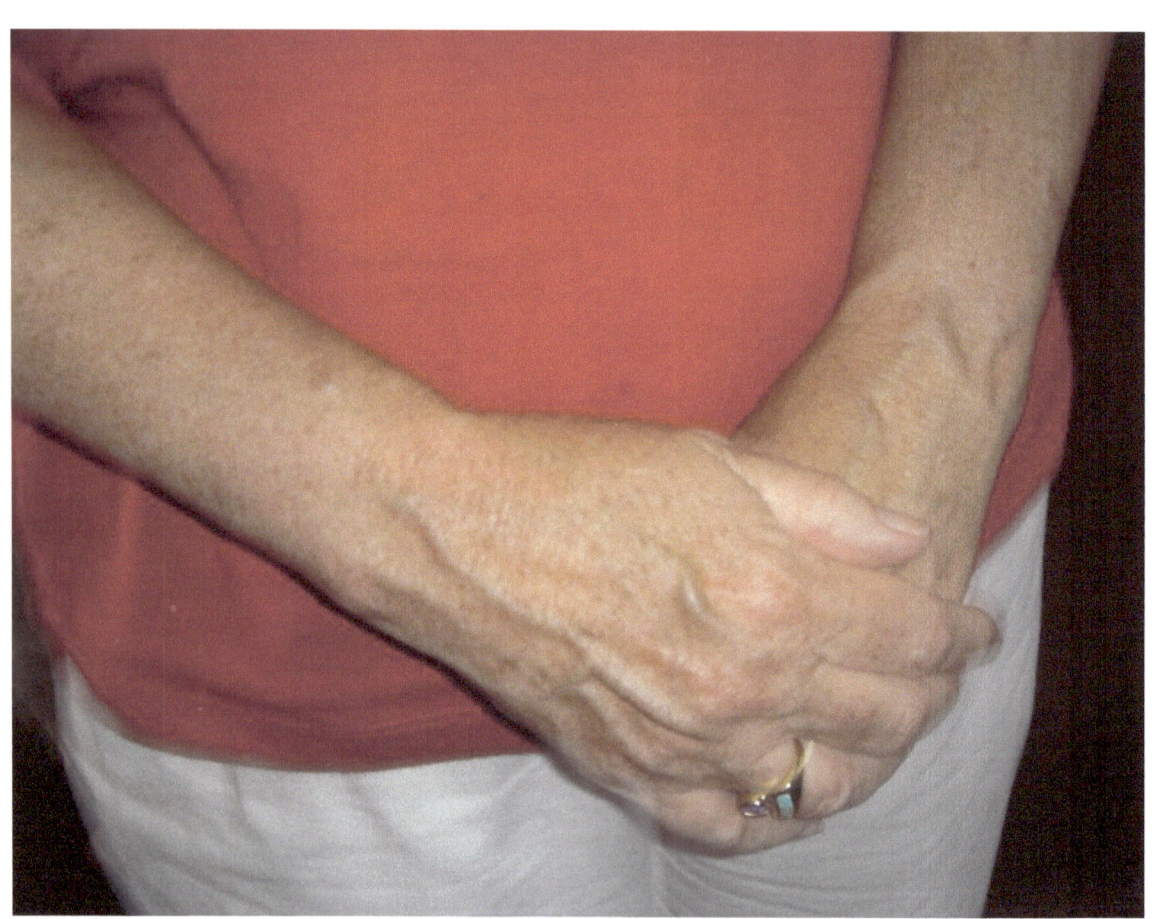

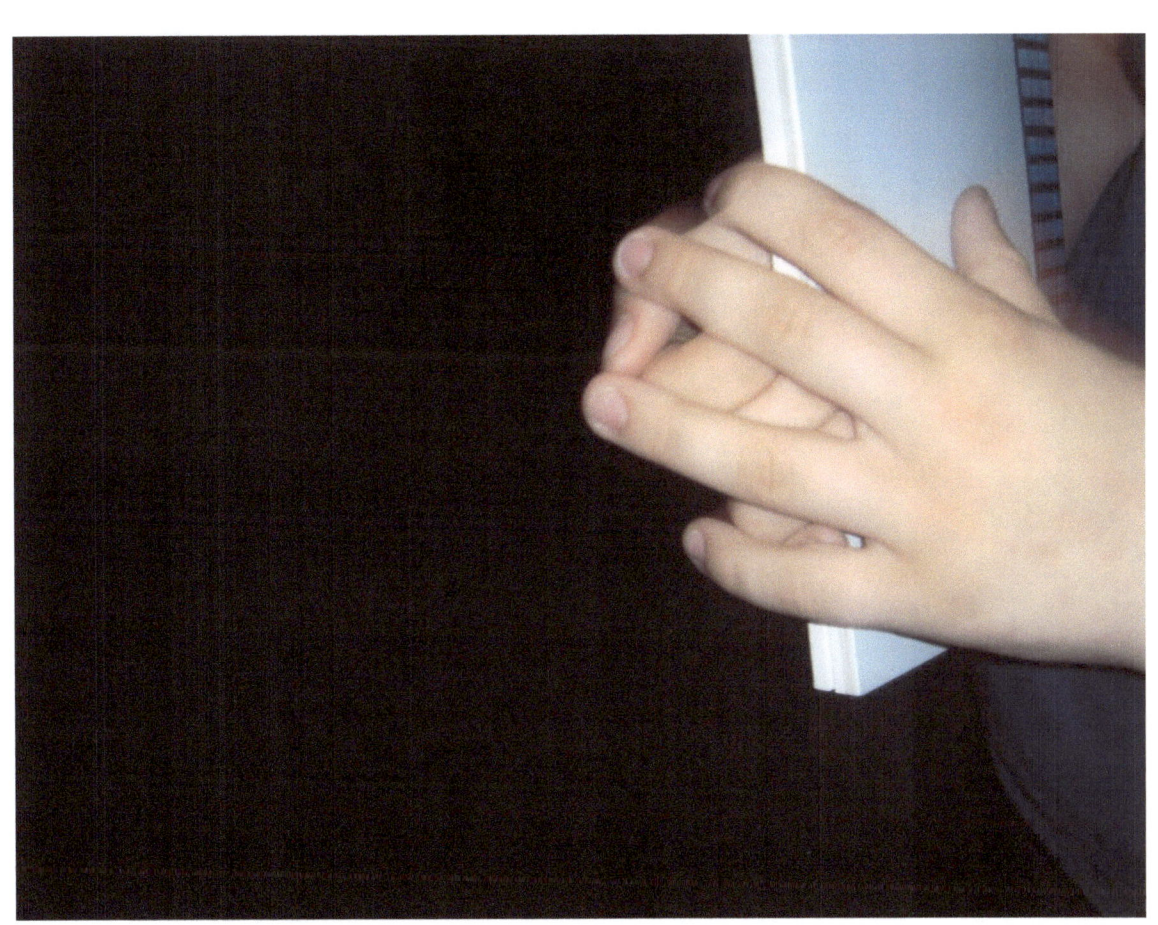

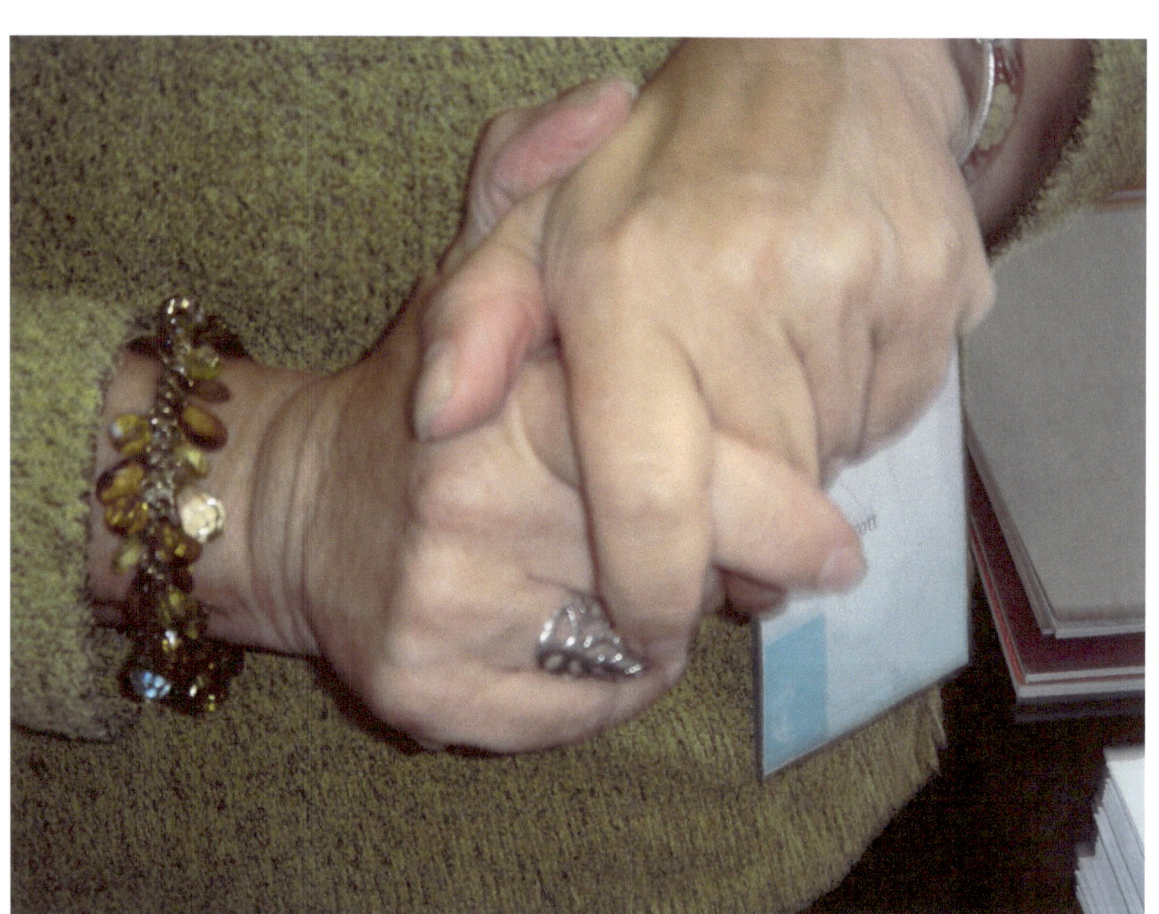

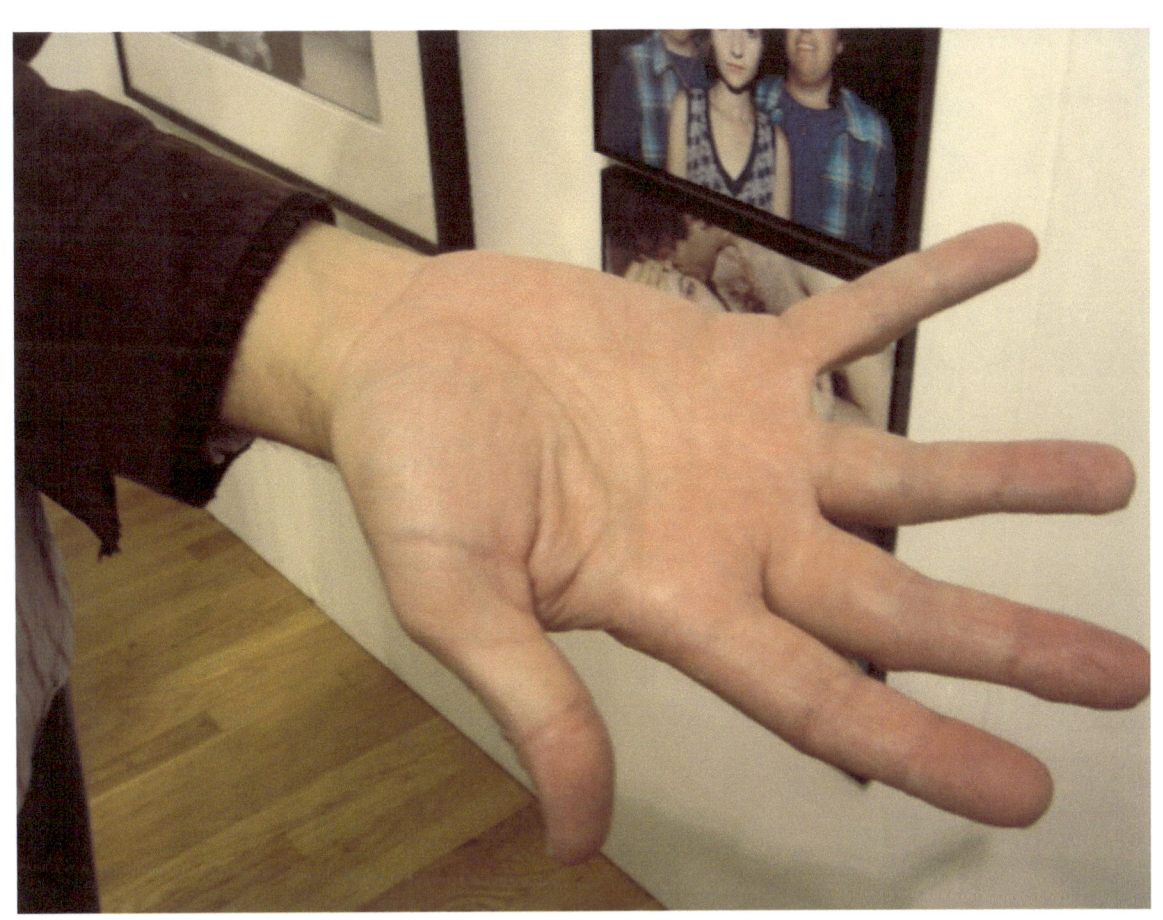

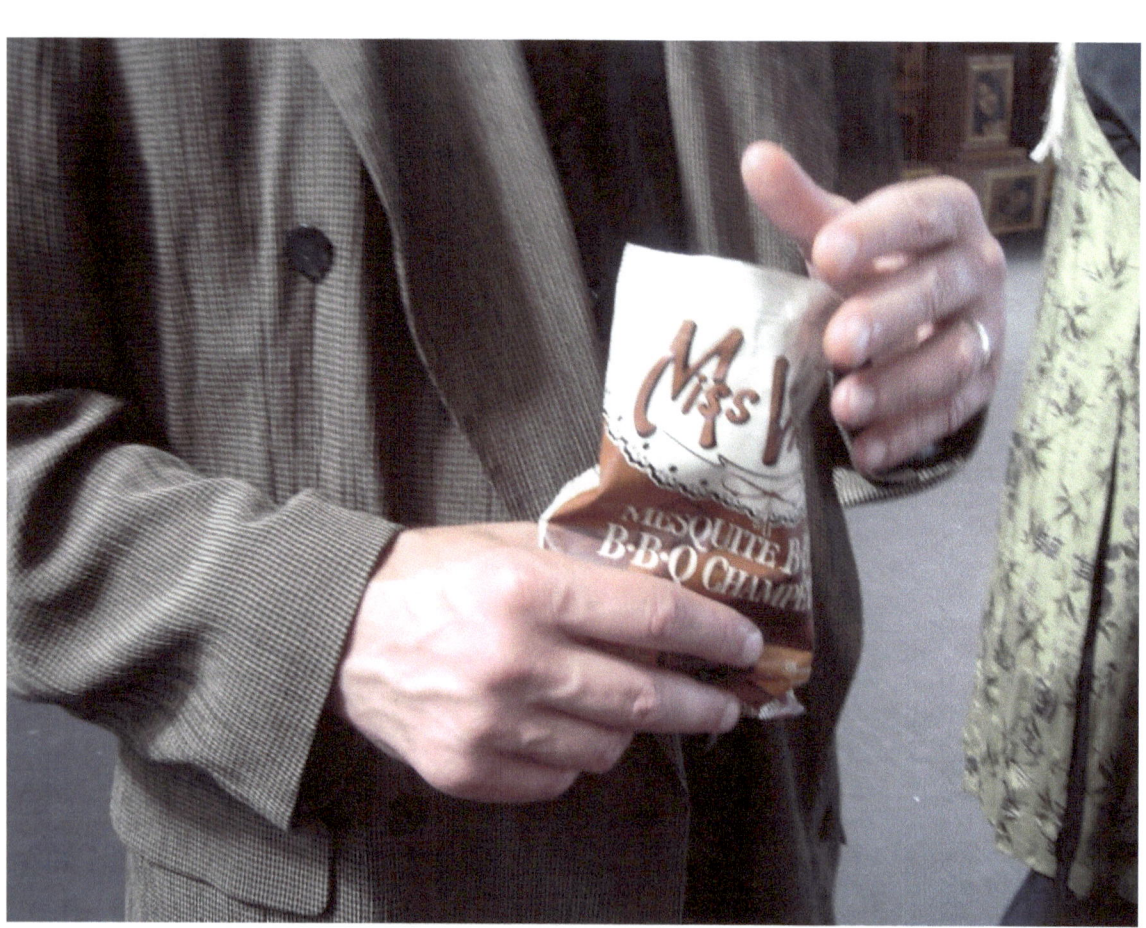

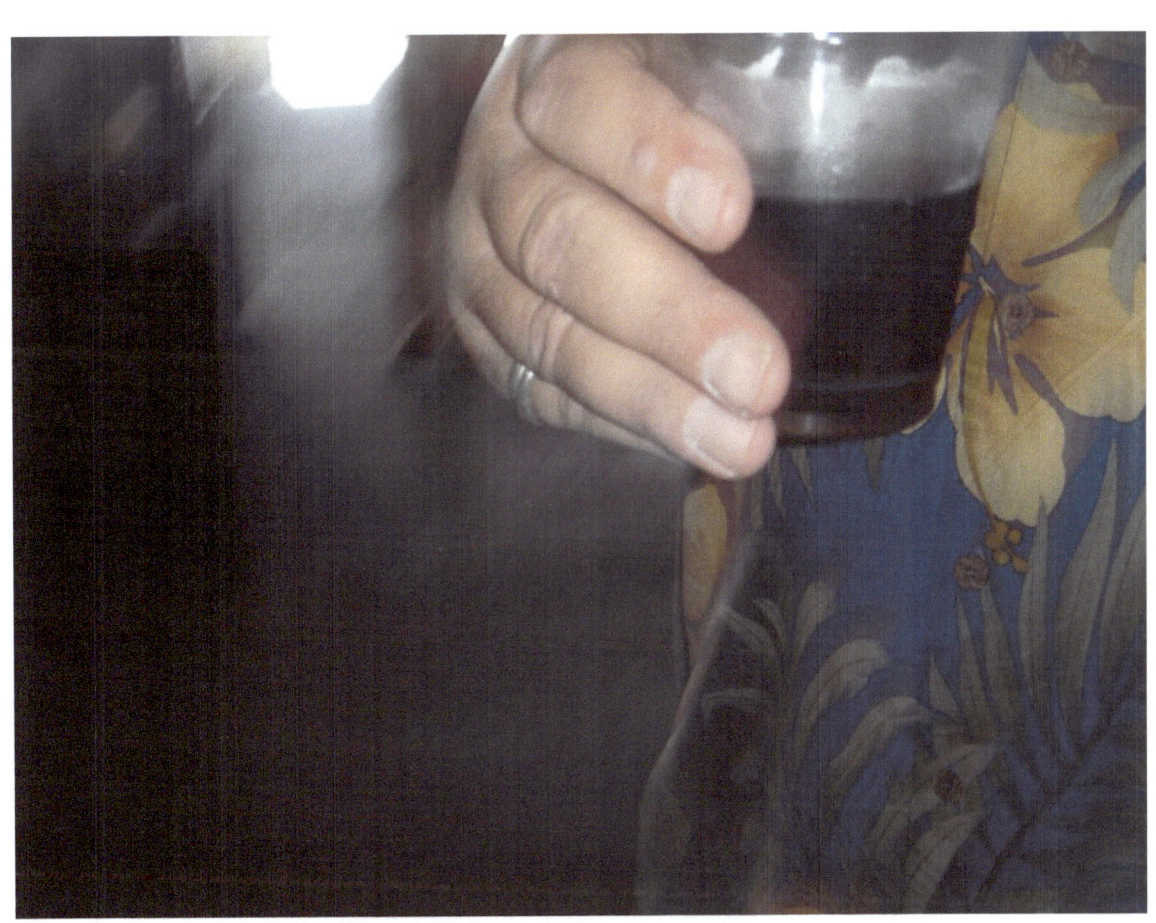

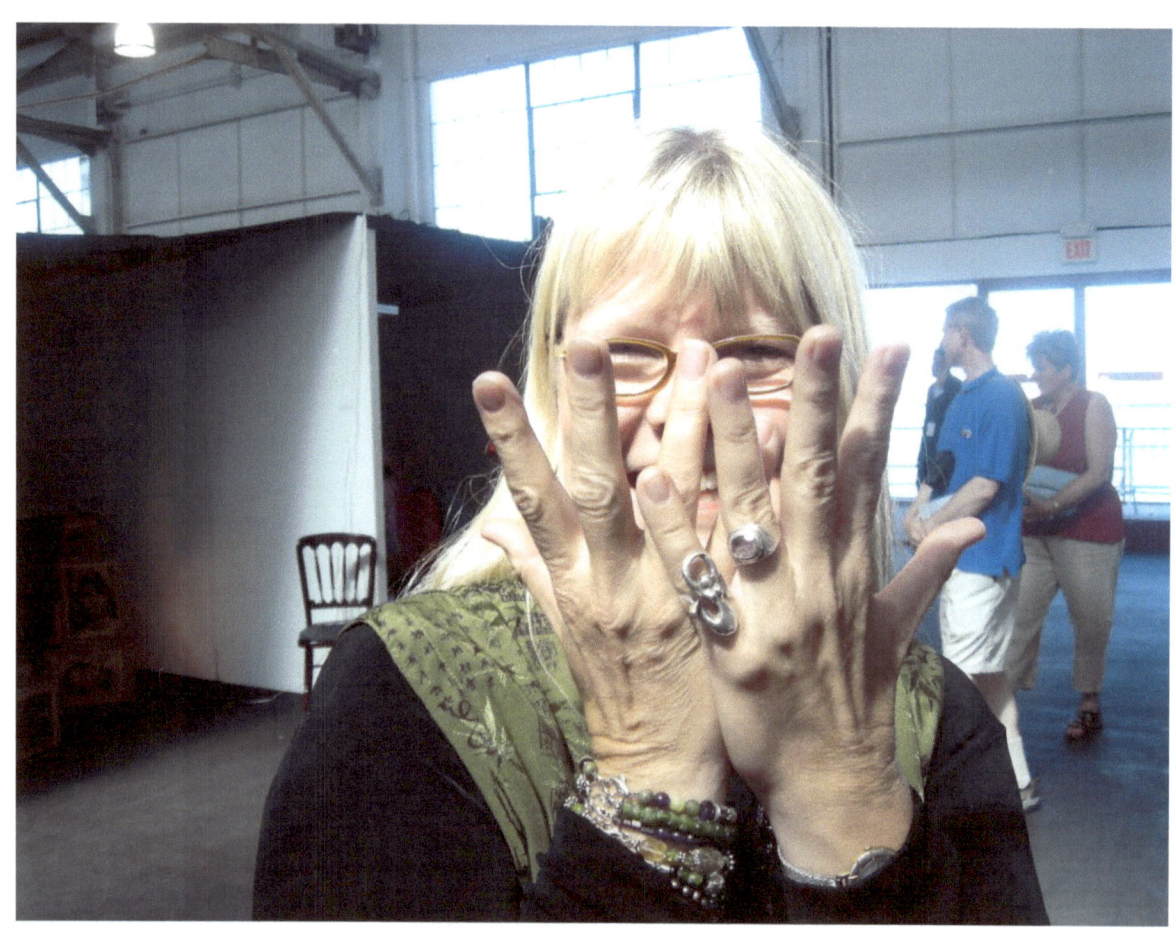

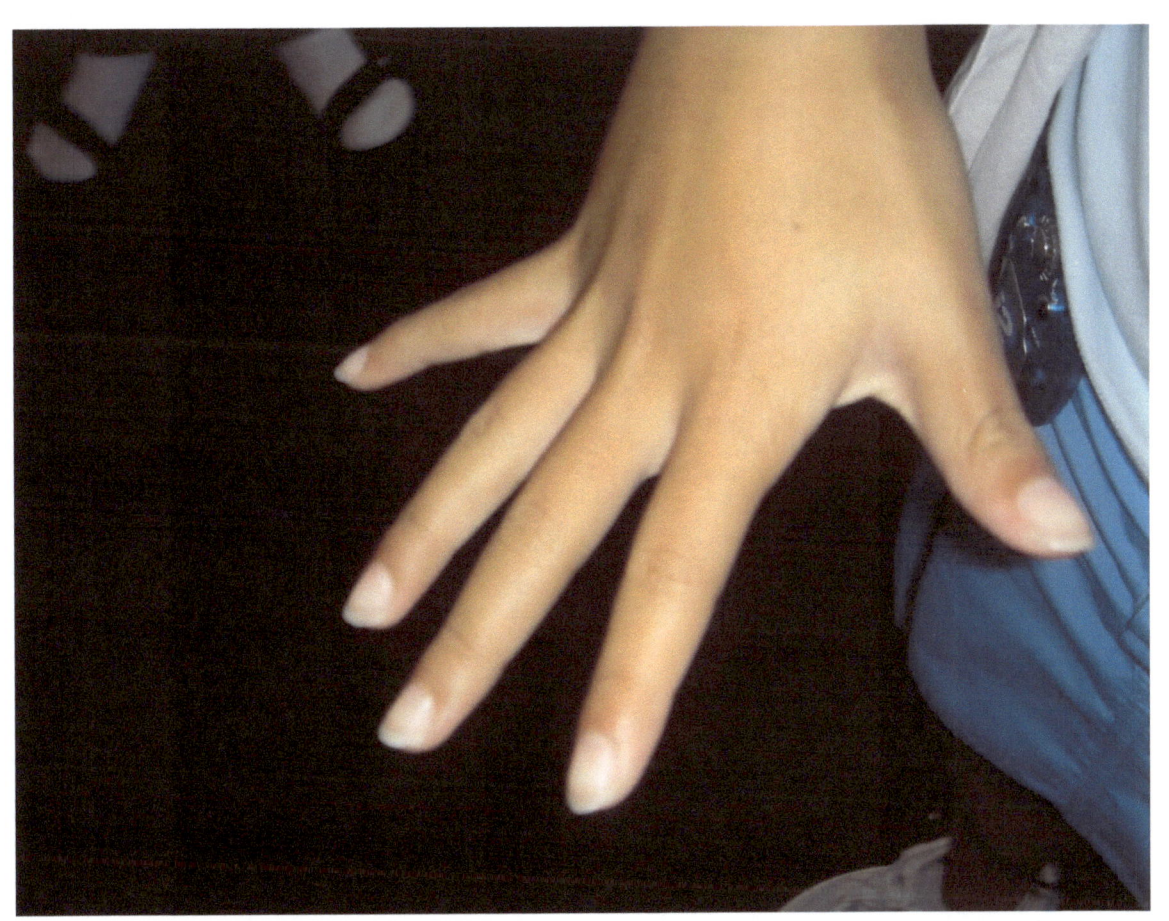

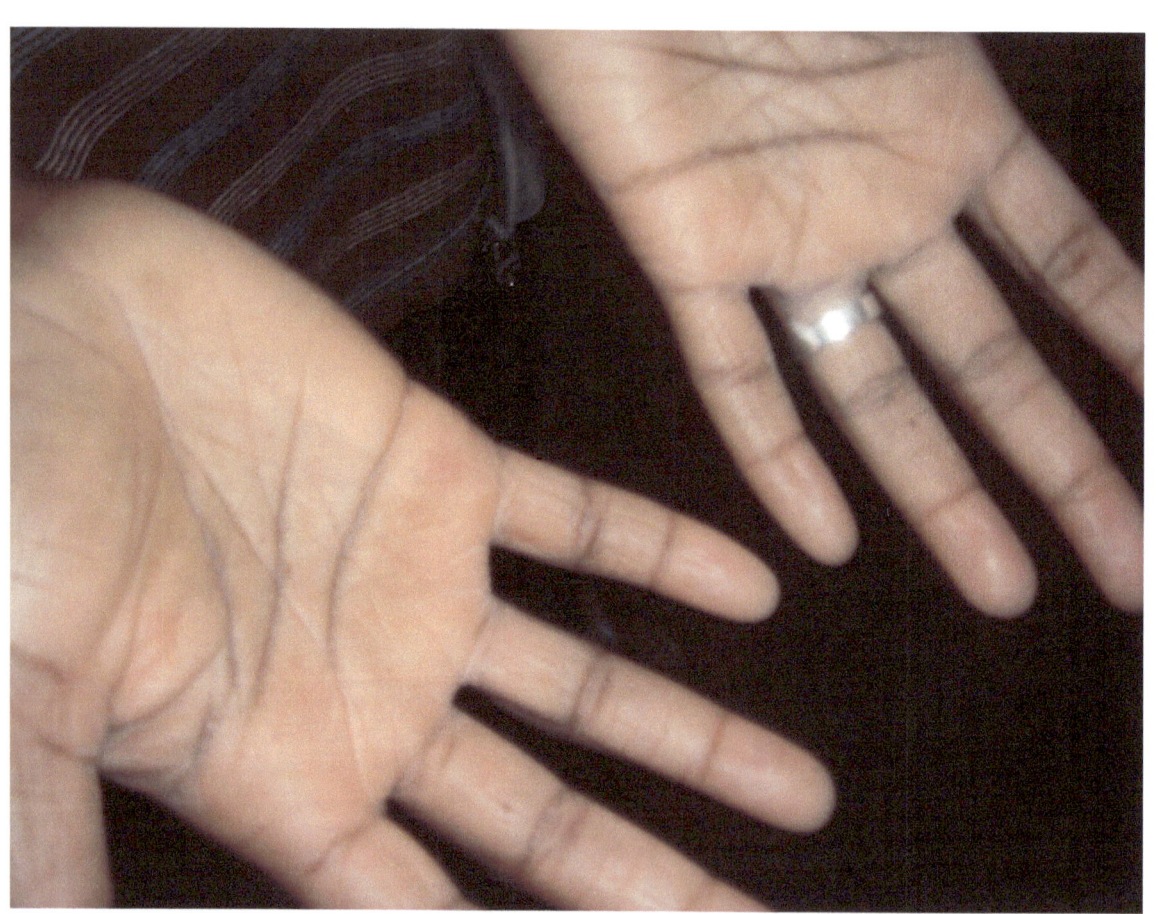

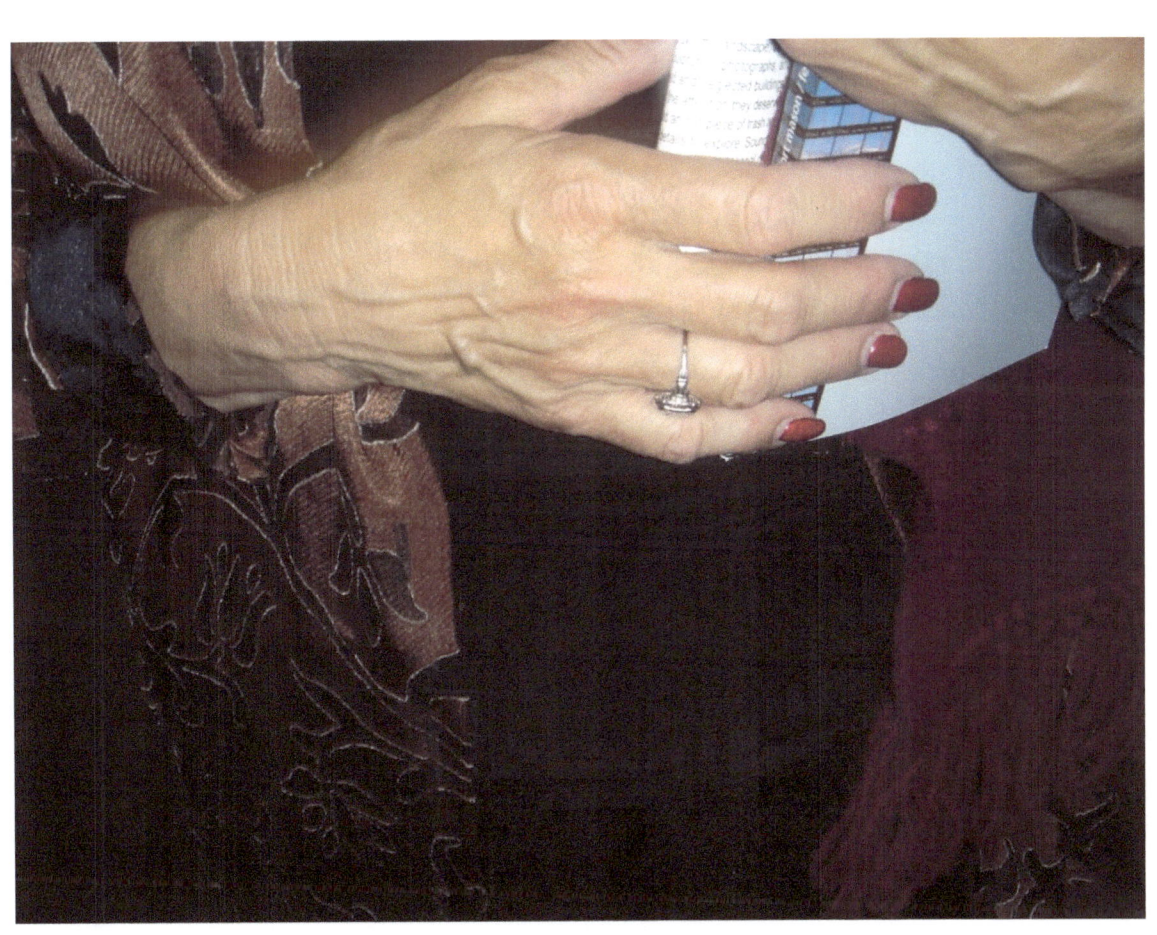

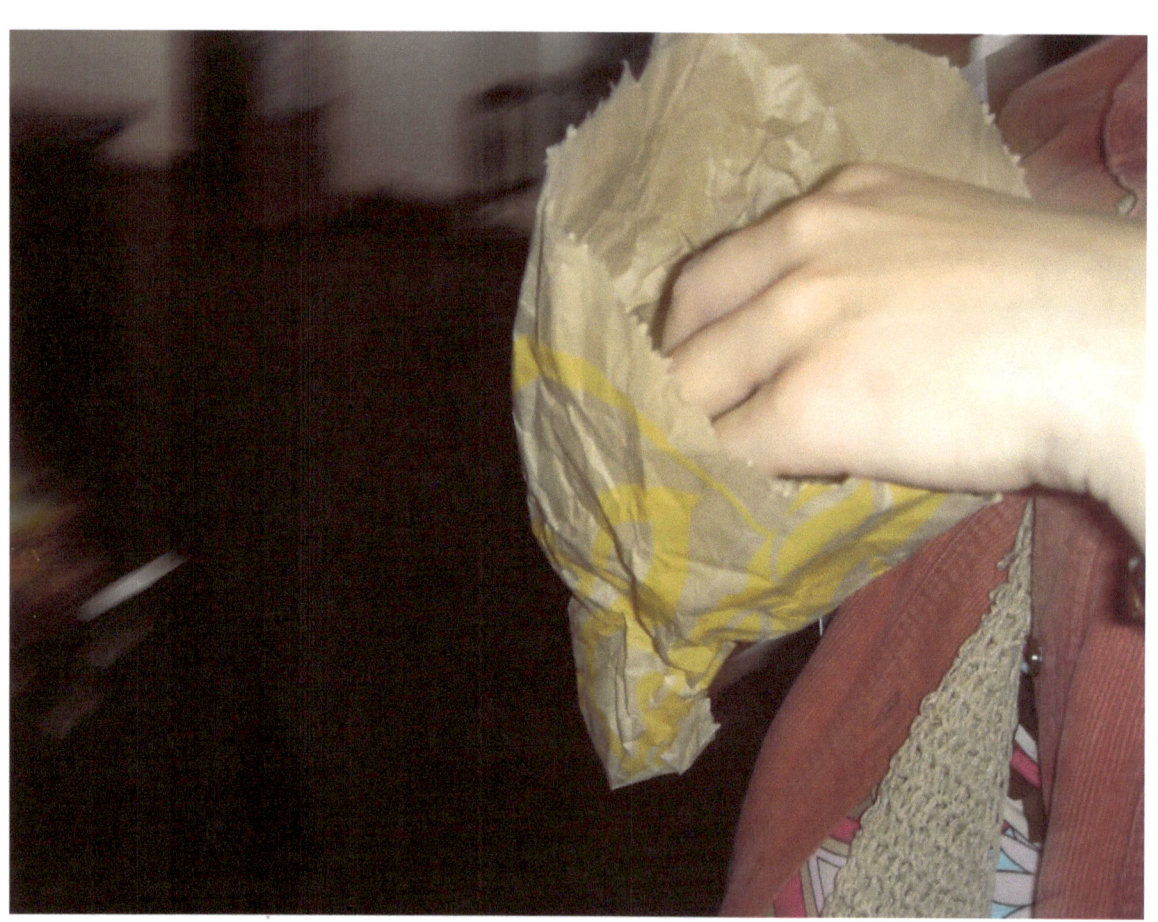

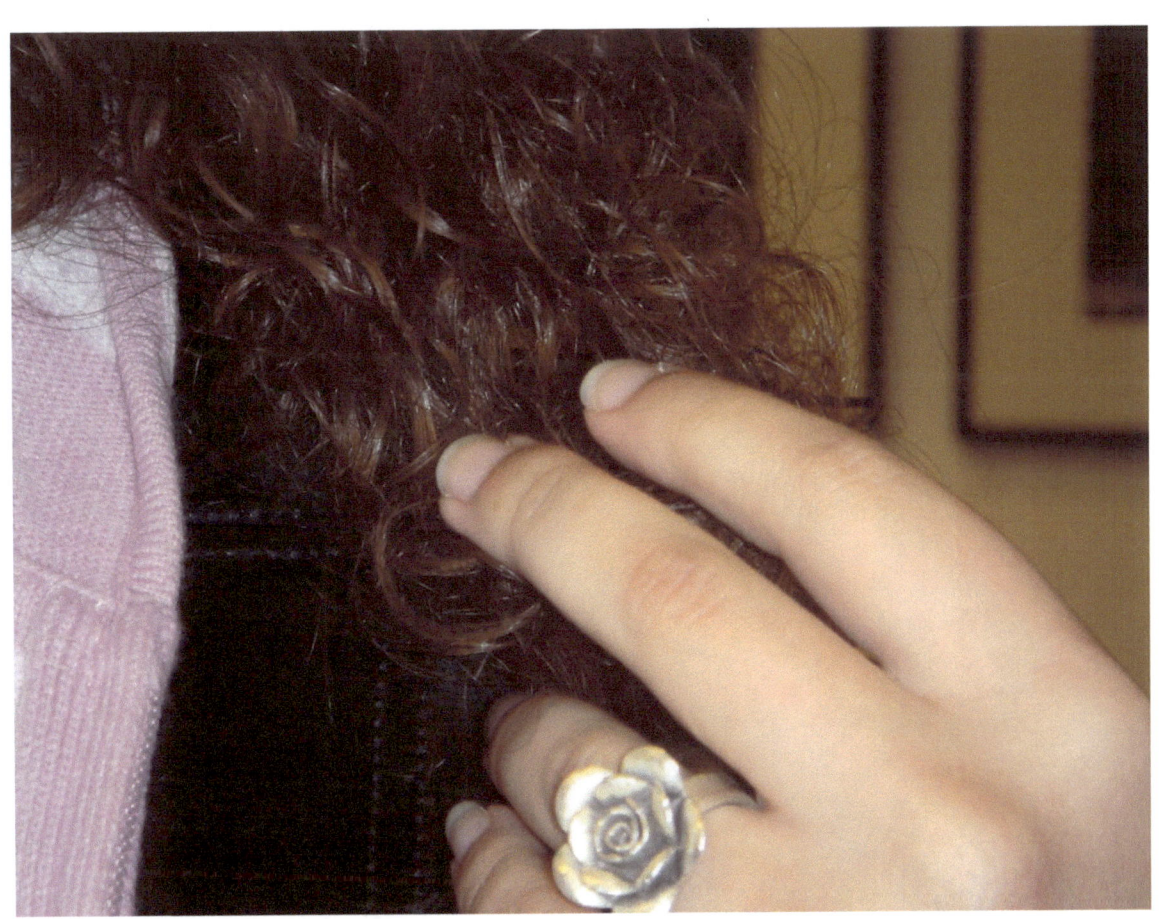

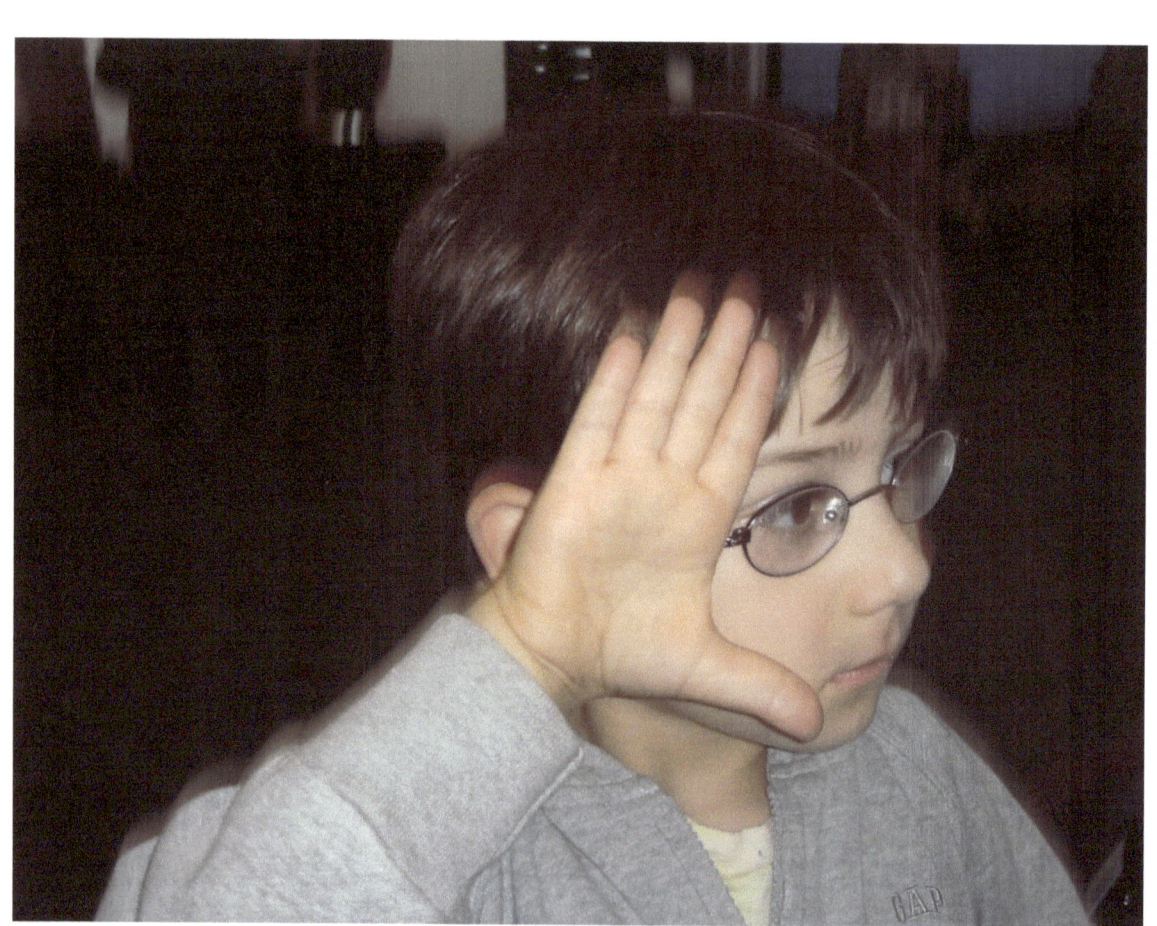

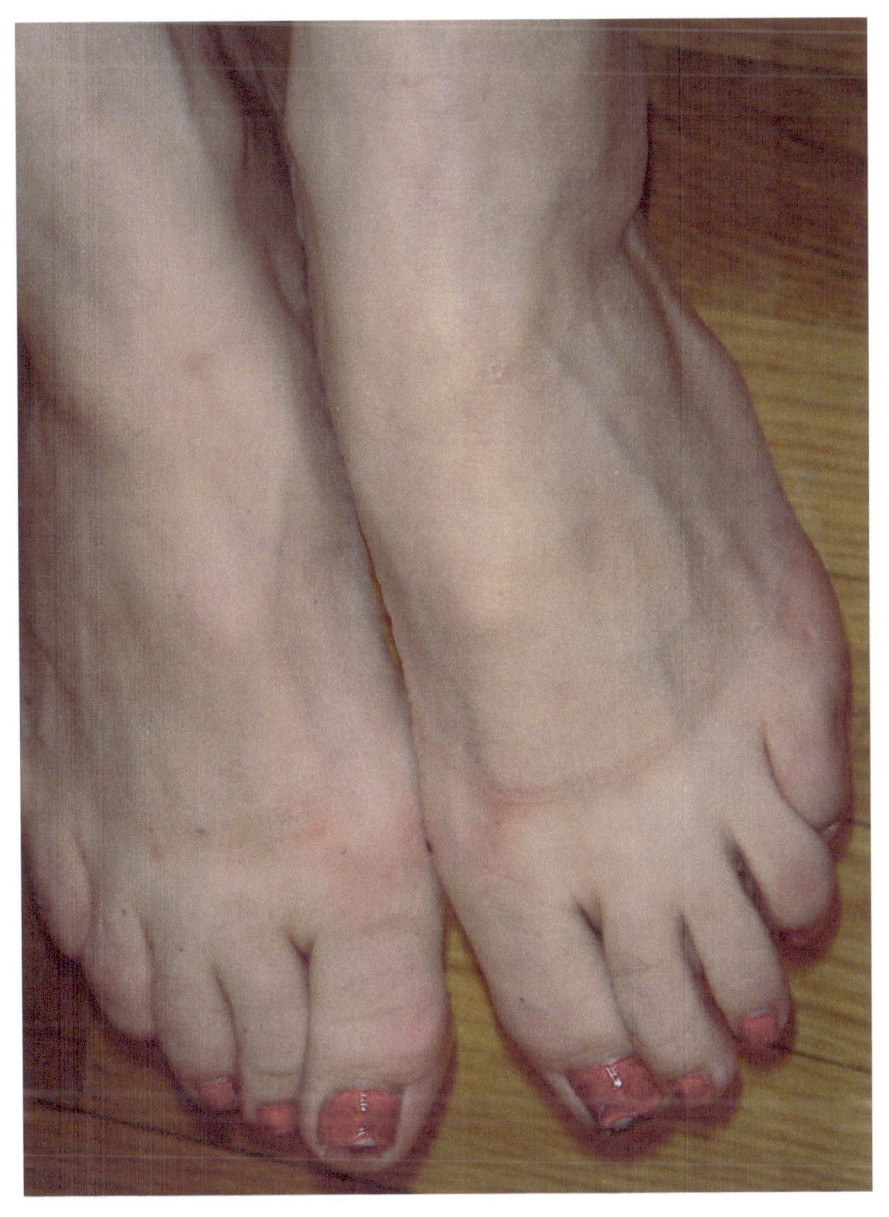

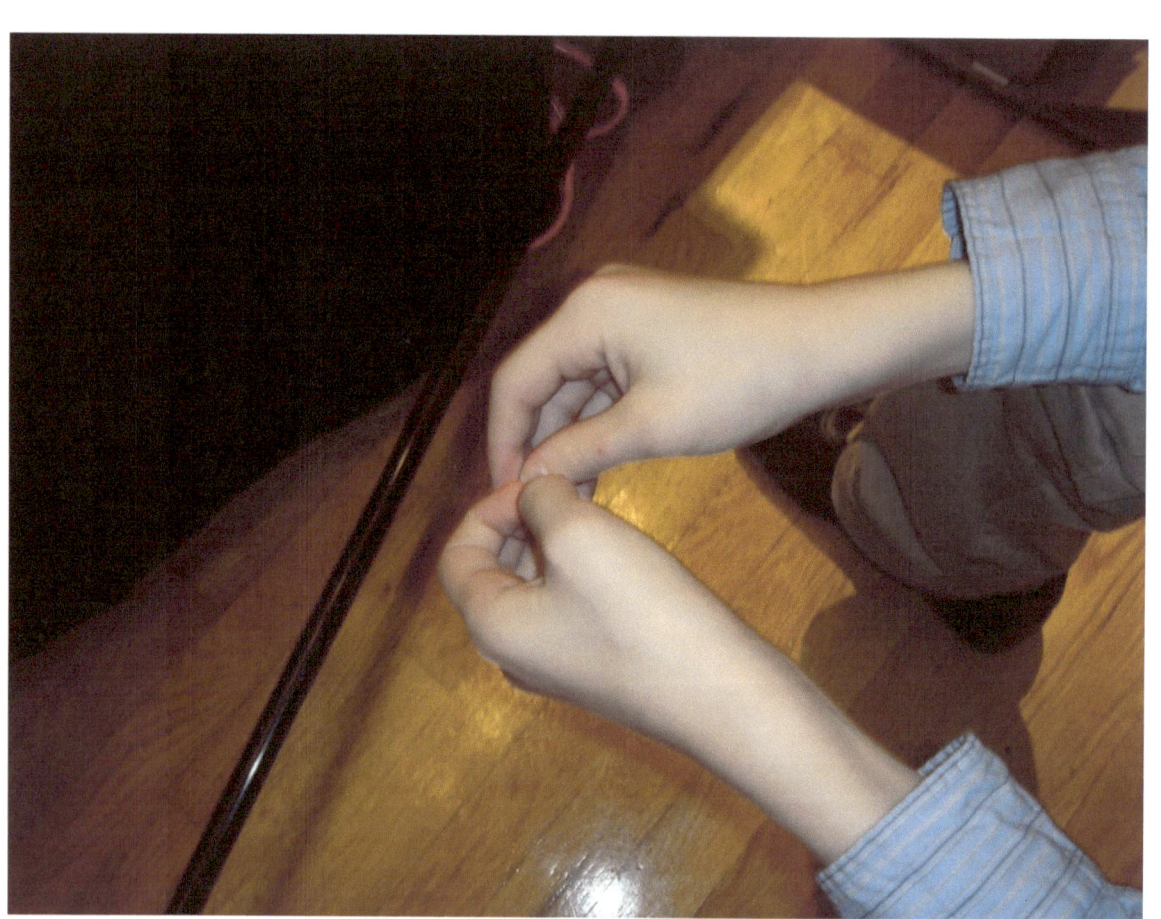

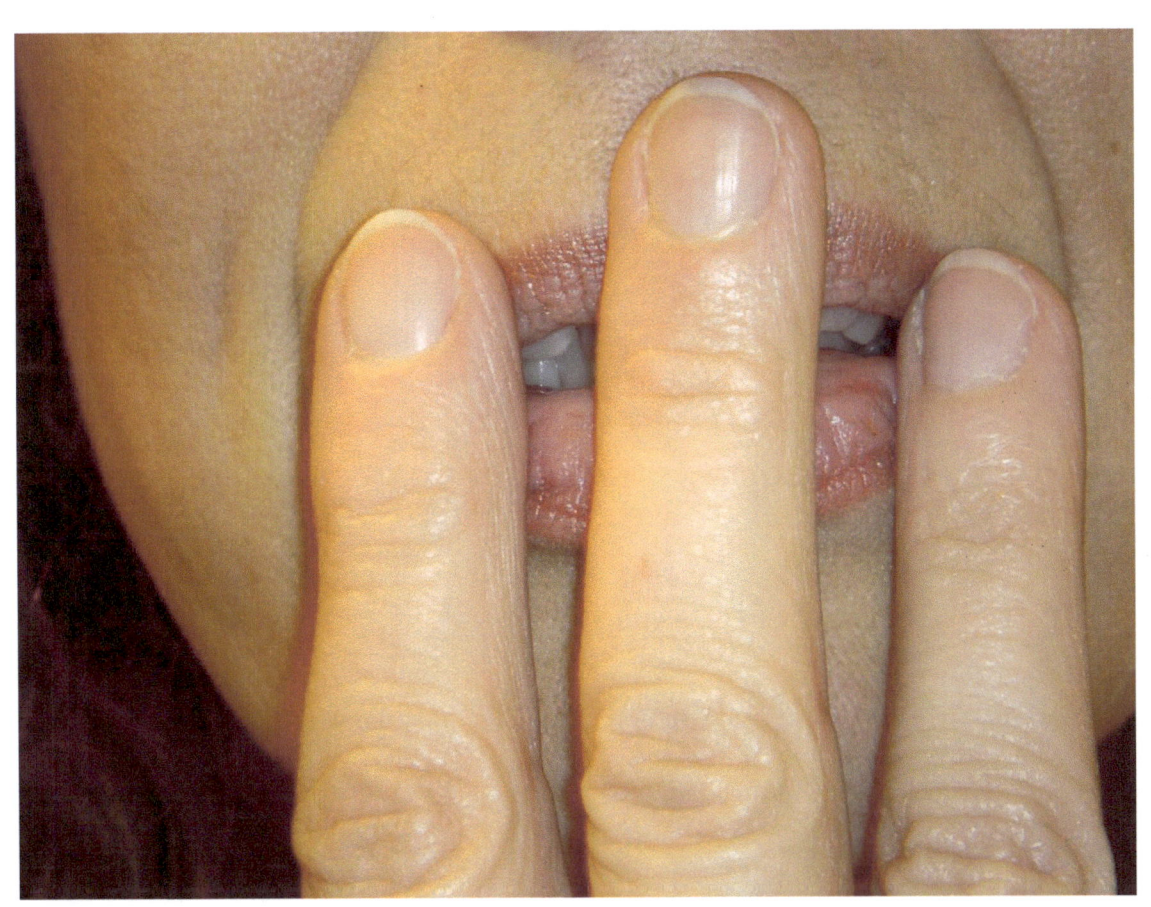

www.ingramcontent.com/pod-product-compliance
Lightning Source LLC
Chambersburg PA
CBHW050732180526
45159CB00003B/1205